GEORGE ELIOT

George Eliot was born Mary A
1819, near Nuneaton, Warwick:
Evangelist, and received a classi
schools. After the death of her m
Coventry with her father and beca   ..ce-
thinkers Charles and Cara Bray, w   _ ω ner translating
Strauss' *Life of Jesus* (1846). After her father's death in 1849, she
moved to London, where she met George Henry Lewes, who was
separated from, but crucially unable to divorce, his wife. Moving
to Germany with him in 1854, she lived as his common-law wife
for twenty-four years. Under his encouragement she began
writing fiction under her nom de plume: the successful serial
Scenes of Clerical Life (1858); the best-selling *Adam Bede*
(1859); followed by a number of poems and further highly
praised works such as *The Mill on the Floss* (1860), *Silas Marner*
(1861), *Middlemarch* (1871–2) and *Daniel Deronda* (1876).
Lewes' death in 1878 saw the effective devastation of her writing
career. A few short months into her marriage to a man twenty
years her junior, she died in December 1880.

HELEN EDMUNDSON

Helen Edmundson's first play, *Flying*, was presented at the
National Theatre Studio in 1990. In 1992, she adapted Tolstoy's
Anna Karenina for Shared Experience, for whom she also
adapted *The Mill on the Floss* in 1994. Both won awards – the
TMA and the Time Out Awards respectively – and both
productions were twice revived and extensively toured. Shared
Experience also staged her adaptation of *War and Peace* at the
National Theatre in 1996 and on tour in a revised two-part
version in 2008, and toured her adaptations of Mary Webb's
Gone to Earth in 2004 and Euripides' *Orestes* in 2006. Her
original play *The Clearing* was first staged at The Bush Theatre
in 1993, winning John Whiting and Time Out Awards, and
Mother Teresa is Dead was premiered at the Royal Court Theatre
in 2002. Her adaptation of Jamila Gavin's *Coram Boy* premiered
at the National Theatre to critical acclaim in 2005, receiving a
Time Out Award. It was subsequently revived in 2006, and
produced on Broadway in 2007.

Other Adaptations in this Series

AFTER MRS ROCHESTER
Polly Teale
*Based on the life and work
     of* Jean Rhys

ANIMAL FARM
Ian Wooldridge
Adapted from George Orwell

ANNA KARENINA
Helen Edmundson
Adapted from Leo Tolstoy

ARABIAN NIGHTS
Dominic Cooke

BEAUTY AND THE BEAST
Laurence Boswell

BRONTË
Polly Teale
*Based on the life and work
     of the* Brontës

THE CANTERBURY TALES
Mike Poulton
Adapted from Geoffrey Chaucer

A CHRISTMAS CAROL
Karen Louise Hebden
Adapted from Charles Dickens

CINDERELLA
Stuart Paterson

CORAM BOY
Helen Edmundson
Adapted from Jamila Gavin

DAVID COPPERFIELD
Alastair Cording
Adapted from Charles Dickens

DR JEKYLL AND MR HYDE
David Edgar
Adapted from Robert Louis Stevenson

EMMA
Martin Millar and Doon MacKichan
Adapted from Jane Austen

FAR FROM THE MADDING CROWD
Mark Healy
Adapted from Thomas Hardy

GONE TO EARTH
Helen Edmundson
Adapted from Mary Webb

GREAT EXPECTATIONS
Nick Ormerod and Declan Donnellan
Adapted from Charles Dickens

HANSEL AND GRETEL
Stuart Paterson

JANE EYRE
Polly Teale
Adapted from Charlotte Brontë

THE JUNGLE BOOK
Stuart Paterson
Adapted from Rudyard Kipling

KENSUKE'S KINGDOM
Stuart Paterson
Adapted from Michael Morpurgo

KES
Lawrence Till
Adapted from Barry Hines

MADAME BOVARY
Fay Weldon
Adapted from Gustave Flaubert

MARY BARTON
Rona Munro
Adapted from Elizabeth Gaskell

NORTHANGER ABBEY
Tim Luscombe
Adapted from Jane Austen

SLEEPING BEAUTY
Rufus Norris

SUNSET SONG
Alastair Cording
Adapted from
     Lewis Grassic Gibbon

TREASURE ISLAND
Stuart Paterson
Adapted from Robert Louis Stevenson

WAR AND PEACE
Helen Edmundson
Adapted from Leo Tolstoy

THE MILL
ON THE FLOSS

adapted from George Eliot's novel by

Helen Edmundson

wih a Foreword by Claire Tomalin

NICK HERN BOOKS
London
www.nickhernbooks.co.uk

A Nick Hern Book

This adaptation of *The Mill on the Floss* first published in Great Britain in 1994 as a paperback original by Nick Hern Books Limited, 14 Larden Road, London W3 7ST

Reprinted 2001, 2008

The Mill on the Floss copyright © 1994 Helen Edmundson

Helen Edmundson has asserted her right to be identified as the author of this work

Foreword copyright © Claire Tomalin

Front cover photo: Mike Kwasniak

Typeset by Country Setting, Kingsdown, Kent CT14 8ES
Printed in the UK by CPI Antony Rowe, Chippenham, Wiltshire

A CIP catalogue record for this book is available from the British Library

ISBN 978 1 85459 276 7

FSC

Mixed Sources
Product group from well-managed
forests and other controlled sources

Cert no. SGS-COC-2953
www.fsc.org
© 1996 Forest Stewardship Council

George Eliot

by Claire Tomalin

George Eliot was born in 1819, the same year as the future
Queen Victoria: only she was not born 'George Eliot' of
course, but Mary Ann Evans. Her father was a Warwickshire
estate manager earning a modest but comfortable living, and
she went to school in Nuneaton and Coventry and was seen to
be outstandingly clever, certainly more so than her much-loved
brother Isaac. When she was sixteen their mother died and she
left school, though continuing to study with tutors; then her
older sister married, and she became her father's housekeeper.
As Mr Tulliver says of his daughter Maggie at the beginning of
The Mill on the Floss, being so clever does no harm to a little
girl, but once grown up, 'an over-cute woman's no better nor a
long-tailed sheep – she'll fetch none the bigger price for that.'

But Mary Ann Evans did grow up to fetch a big price, if not in
the way Mr Tulliver meant it. By the time she was forty – her
age when *The Mill on the Floss* was published – she had
become one of the most highly acclaimed novelists of the
nineteenth century. And although her readers gradually found
out that she was not a man at all, she will always be remembered by the masculine name she used for her books, just as
her French contemporary Aurore Dudevant is known by her
literary name of George Sand. Both women, as well as being
formidably clever, were rebels too, and prepared to defy the
conventions of their society. Still, when it came to appearing in
print, they chose to disguise themselves as men, as the Bronte
sisters also did.

In Mary Ann Evans case there was good reason for the disguise. She had brought disgrace on the family name of Evans
by living in sin with a married man. George Henry Lewes was
a journalist and scientific writer who had made a 'free' marriage
and then found himself saddled with a wife who kept producing
children by her lover, while expecting Lewes to maintain her
and them. Lewes was wretched but, although separated, could

not get a divorce; and in 1854 Miss Evans, who had endured several painful experiences of her own with men, decided she loved him enough to dispense with formalities.

They went abroad together, announcing the fact to their close friends, and then returned and settled in London. Although she called herself 'Mrs Lewes', they never pretended to be married, and agreed to have no children, she became a good and generous stepmother to his sons. This was the high noon of Victorian decorum in sexual matters – in public at any rate – and her behaviour made her a social outcast for some time. Her brother broke off all contact with her and many of her friends were scandalised. In spite of this the relationship was entirely happy and fulfilling to both parties, and it was Lewes who encouraged her to try her hand at fiction.

It was also Lewes who found her a publisher for her first book of stories, *Scenes from Clerical Life*. He clearly took some sly pleasure in leading the publisher to believe that the new author for whom he was acting was a clergyman, and explained that he was ambitious but very shy and shrinking – too shy to meet anyone, or even to correspond directly with his own publisher. Lewes allowed her to invent her own false name; she used his George as a loving tribute, and added Eliot as 'a good mouth-filling, easily pronounced word'. And among her first readers and admirers, only Dickens guessed that this was the work of a woman, because he thought no man could have written about children and domestic details so convincingly.

Eliot was popular from the beginning, and 'his' next book, *Adam Bede*, a full length novel, was still more of a success. It was read with great enthusiasm by Queen Victoria, and particularly praised for its moral lessons. Inevitably there was more speculation about the identity of the author and Lewes and Evans both found themselves forced to lie directly when questioned by friends who suspected the truth. When it did finally come out, Lewes stated that the reason for the subterfuge had been simply to get the book judged on its merits, 'and not prejudged as the work of a woman'. He added defiantly, 'they can't now unsay their admiration'. In fact some did turn round and declare that the moral teaching could not have any force once it was known that it came from an immoral woman or 'polluted source', as the owner of Mudie's Select Library, a very important distributor, put it.

Still George Eliot faced out the critics and triumphed. T*he Mill on the Floss* was her third book, and although some critics objected to its frank description of physical attraction, it has been a favourite from the beginning with those who enjoy its intensities of feeling. It contained a partial self-portrait in Maggie Tulliver who is dark, disobedient and passionate, and leads an imaginative life at odds with the simple provincial world into which she is born. The difference between Maggie and Mary Ann is that Maggie is never allowed to escape, and one way of reading her story is to see it as Mary Ann Evans, the moralist, punishing Maggie Tulliver for her own sins of rebelliousness and passion. In the novel, little Maggie cuts off her hair in a rage and runs away to the gypsies; growing up, she allows herself to be wooed by her cousin's intended husband, and turns to self-sacrifice for her redemption. In real life, Mary Ann had distressed her father by refusing to go to church when she stopped believing, made her intellectual escape through friendship with free thinkers with advanced social ideas, and educated herself to the highest levels of scholarship. The difference is marked.

George Eliot went on to greater triumphs, especially with the fable of *Silas Marner* and her masterpiece, *Middlemarch*, which again draws on the provincial society she remembered from her childhood. She came to be regarded with something approaching awe in English society, and was particularly revered by women; several who fought for the rights of their sex were among her friends, including Barbara Bodichon, Emily Davies (who founded Girton College) and Octavia Hill. Yet Eliot never joined actively in their movement, and both in her work and her life she showed that dependence on a loved man was at least as important to her as the forging of her own path.

She is not a feminist writer in the sense that she proposed new goals for women; on the other hand there is an unmistakable feminist element in her writing, and especially in her sympathy for characters like Maggie Tulliver and Dorothea Brooke who feel the cruel lack of education and opportunity and would like to do something more in the world than they are permitted. There is also a strongly expressed belief in the good qualities she ascribes to women, their kindness, their self-denial, their intuitive sympathies. Some readers accept this, others question whether these qualities are necessarily inherent in one sex.

Eliot was a pioneer but also a self-doubter. She suffered from ill health and depression all through her adult life. She needed constant reassurance and support from Lewes, who always hid bad reviews and often 'mislaid' any letters he thought might upset her. When he died, to everyone's amazement, she immediately accepted a proposal of marriage from a family friend, John Cross, twenty years younger than her, his mother had died at the same time as Lewes, and he called her 'Aunt'. Her friends were dismayed again, but news of the marriage brought the first communication for 25 years from her brother Isaac – such was the magic of respectability at last. She did not live more than a few months to enjoy it, at the end of 1880, she was dead. Isaac appeared among the mourners in Highgate Cemetery, and Cross wrote a biography which contrived to leave out just about everything that made her interesting. As so often, Virginia Woolf summed up the contradictions in Eliot's nature when she described her 'shuddering back into the arms of love as if there alone were satisfaction and, it might be, justification, at the same time reaching out with "a fastidious yet hungry ambition" for all that life could offer the free and inquiring mind and confronting her feminine aspirations with the real world of men'. Perhaps the most important thing about her is that she saw the world honestly and finely, and drew unforgettable pictures of people going about their daily activities and worrying over the dilemmas into which they are drawn by greed, ambition and love. These are things which do not change, and even at the end of the twentieth century her characters and their problems are still fully recognisable.

Claire Tomalin is an author jounalist, critic and playwright. Her most recent publication is The Invisible Woman – the Story of Nellie Turner and Charles Dickens.

Author's Note

This play was written to be performed on a stage with two levels. It could, however, be performed on a single-level stage, as long as the space would allow for simultaneous action in two areas, and an alternative method of 'ducking the witch' could be found.

Although the play is split into scenes, this is more for the benefit of director and actor in rehearsal. Wherever possible, the action of each scene should flow into the next (indeed, this is sometimes demanded by the text). Care should be taken, however, where identical characters are used in consecutive scenes, to delineate any changes of place or movement of time.

Helen Edmundson

The Mill on the Floss was first performed by Shared Experience Theatre Company in association with the Wolsey Theatre, Ipswich on 17 March 1994 with the following cast:

MR TULLIVER, DR KENN   Simeon Andrews

FIRST MAGGIE   Shirley Henderson

BOB JAKIN, PHILLIP WAKEM, UNCLE PULLET
                                        Michael Matus

SECOND MAGGIE, AUNT GLEGG   Buddug Morgan

TOM TULLIVER, WAKEM   Ian Puleston-Davies

STEPHEN GUEST, MR STELLING, UNCLE GLEGG
                                        Simon Robson

MRS TULLIVER, LUCY DEANE   Clara Salaman

THIRD MAGGIE, AUNT PULLET   Helen Schlesinger

Directed by Nancy Meckler and Polly Teale

Designed by Bunny Christie

Music composed by Peter Salem

Lighting by Chris Davey

Movement by Liz Ranken

Scene One

Music.

Lights up on FIRST MAGGIE. *She is standing still on the bank, book in hand, staring at the river. The air is full of the sound of the water rushing through the mill wheel. Above the noise we hear a woman's voice (her mother) calling*

Maggie. Maggie.

But MAGGIE *does not respond. Instead, she sits cross-legged, and begins to read her book. On the upper platform, dimly lit, the characters of the play gather as a crowd.*

MAGGIE. '. . . bringing those things called witches or conjurors to justice; this is, first to know if a woman be a witch, throw her into a pond; and if she be a witch she will swim, and it is not in her own power to prevent it . . .'

The crowd, suddenly brightly lit, come to life, as MAGGIE *repeats the words of the book. They gather threateningly around a woman, (similar to* MAGGIE *with long dark hair) haul her aloft and duck her. As she goes under water,* MAGGIE *turns and sees her and, as if she too is under water, struggles to reach her. The woman is hauled out and ducked a second time.* MAGGIE *fights her way towards her but the woman drowns before her eyes.* MAGGIE *screams –*

MAGGIE. No.

The crowd fall silent and stare down at her.

Then they break. MR TULLIVER, MRS TULLIVER *and* MR STELLING *descend and take their places for the next scene. The rest leave.* MAGGIE *goes back to her book.*

Scene Two

MR *and* MRS TULLIVER *and* MR STELLING *sit in the parlour at Dorlcote Mill.*

MR TULLIVER. What I want . . . What I want is to give my son, Tom, a good eddication; an eddication as 'll be a bread to him. All the learnin' my father ever paid for was a bit o' birch at one end and the alphabet at the other. Not that a man can't be an excellent miller and farmer and a shrewd sensible fellow into the bargain, without much help from the schoolmaster . . .

MR STELLING. Oh, I don't doubt it.

MR TULLIVER. But that's just it. I don't want Tom to follow me into the Mill. I want him to be a bit of a scholard, so as he might be up to the tricks o' these fellows as talk fine and write with a flourish. It'ud be a help to me wi' these lawsuits and arbitrations.

MR STELLING. Ah. You wish him to be a lawyer.

MR TULLIVER. A lawyer? Nay, I'll not make a downright lawyer o' the lad. I should be sorry for him to be a raskill.

MRS TULLIVER. Mr Tulliver isn't fond of the lawyers.

MR TULLIVER. No, more of an engineer, or an auctioneer and vallyer; one of them smartish businesses as are all profits and no outlay, only for a big watch-chain and a high stool.

MR STELLING. You are talking to the right man, Sir.

MR TULLIVER. I am?

MR STELLING. I dare say I could prepare your boy for any one of those commendable occupations. Why, you need only say to me, 'I wish my son to know arithmetic' and he would know it.

MR TULLIVER. What's that? 'I wish my son to know 'rithmetic'.

MR STELLING. Or you may say, 'I wish my son to draw', and he would draw. Of course, I would start with Euclid and the Eton Grammar. He would soon have a thorough grasp of etymology and be perfectly au fait with his declensions and conjugations.

MRS TULLIVER. But would you give him seconds o' pudding? For he's such a boy for pudding as never was. Both my children can eat as much victuals as most, thank God.

MR TULLIVER. Hush now, Bessy. There's other things to think on besides pudding. That's the fault I have to find with her; if she see a stick i' the road, she's allays thinkin' she can't step over it. You'd stop me hiring a good waggoner 'cause he'd got a mole on his face.

MRS TULLIVER. Dear heart! When did I iver make objection to a man because he'd got a mole on his face? Or anywhere out of sight, for that matter? I'm sure I'm rether fond o' the moles.

MR TULLIVER. No, no, Bessy. I didn't mean justly the mole; I meant . . . but niver mind. It's puzzlin' work, talking. No, what I'm afraid on is as Tom hasn't got the right sort o' brains for a smart fellow.

MR STELLING. Is the boy stupid?

MRS TULLIVER. No.

MR TULLIVER. No. But I doubt he's a bit slowish. He takes after your family, Bessy.

MRS TULLIVER. Yes, that he does.

MR TULLIVER. He's got a notion o' things out o' door, an a sort o' common-sense, as he'd lay hold o' things by the right handle. But he can't abide the books, and spells all wrong, they tell me. You never hear him say cute things like the little wench. The little 'un takes after my side; she's twice as cute as Tom.

MR STELLING. Is that right?

MR TULLIVER. Oh yes. Too cute for a woman, I'm afraid. It's no mischief much while she's a little 'un, but an over-cute woman's no better nor a long-tailed sheep – she'll fetch none the bigger price for that.

MRS TULLIVER. Yes it is a mischief, for it all runs to naughtiness. How to keep her in a clean pinafore two hours together passes my cunning. I don't know where she is now and it's pretty nigh tea-time. (*She goes to the window and looks out.*) I thought so – sitting at the edge of the water with her book. She'll tumble in and drown some day. (*Rapping on the window.*) Maggie. Maggie.

MR TULLIVER (*quietly to* MR STELLING). It's the wonderful'st thing as I picked the mother from her sisters 'o purpose, 'cause she was a bit weak, like. That's the worse wi' the crossing of breeds: you can never justly calkilate what'll come on't.

MAGGIE *enters, dropping her bonnet on the floor and staring at the visitor.*

MRS TULLIVER. Oh dear, oh dear, Maggie, what are you thinkin' of, to throw your bonnet down there?

MR TULLIVER. Now then, Maggie. This is the Reverend Mr Stelling. He has come to discuss your brother's edication.

MAGGIE. Am I to have an education?

MR TULLIVER. What did I tell you? Cute as can be.

MR STELLING. From what I've been hearing, you have no need of one. I see you have been reading.

MAGGIE. Yes, Sir.

MR TULLIVER. She reads straight off as if she knowed it all beforehand.

MR STELLING. Come here then, little miss and show me your book. (*She goes to him.*) Here are some pictures – can you tell me what they mean?

MAGGIE. I can tell you what they all mean. That's a horrible picture, isn't it? But I can't help looking at it. That woman in the water is a witch – well, they've put her in to find out whether she's a witch or not, and if she swims she's a witch, and if she's drowned, and killed, you know, she's innocent and not a witch, just a poor silly woman. But what good would it do her when she was drowned? I suppose she'd go to heaven and God would make it up to her. And this dreadful blacksmith with his arms akimbo, laughing – he's ugly, isn't he? – I'll tell you what he is. He's the devil really. The devil takes the shape of wicked men, mostly blacksmiths because if people saw he was the devil and he roared at them, they'd run away and he couldn't make 'em do what he wanted.

MR STELLING. Well!

MRS TULLIVER. God bless us.

MR TULLIVER. Why, what book is it the wench has got hold on?

MR STELLING. 'The History of the Devil', by Daniel Defoe. Not quite the right book for a little girl.

MR TULLIVER. Did you ever hear the like on't? It's a pity but what she'd been the lad. She'd a been a match for the lawyers, she would.

MR STELLING. She certainly has a way with words.

MR TULLIVER. Now, what about Tom? You can knock him into shape?

MAGGIE. Father, is it a long way off where Tom is to go?

MR TULLIVER. What? Worrying already that you won't have your brother? She fair worships him, you know?

MR STELLING. O, a long, long way off. You must borrow the seven- leagued boots to reach him.

MAGGIE. That's nonsense.

MRS TULLIVER. Maggie! But is it so far off as I couldn't wash and mend him?

MR STELLING. About fifteen miles, that's all.

MRS TULLIVER. Too far for the linen, I doubt.

MR STELLING. I would suggest that you take some time to think it over, Mr Tulliver, but I have had other propositions from interested parties and I can only accommodate one boy – two at the most.

MR TULLIVER. Interested parties, eh?

MR STELLING. One of them is a neighbour of yours. You may know him; a lawyer by the name of Wakem.

MR TULLIVER. Wakem? Wakem?

MRS TULLIVER. Mr Tulliver isn't fond o' Mr Wakem.

MR TULLIVER. I've just gone into arbitration with a client o' Wakem's.

MR STELLING. I'm sorry, I didn't realise . . .

MR TULLIVER. Don't you be sorry. I'll cut his comb for him. I'll show him there are other folk as know how to handle the law. They can't try telling me that this errigation nonsense upstream won't stop my mill. If you've got a mill, you must have water to turn it. Water's a very particular thing. You can't pick it up with a pitchfork but you can steal it all the same, eh Maggie? And Wakem's just the sort of raskill to side with a thief.

MRS TULLIVER. Dear heart, I'm sure Mr Stelling hasn't the time for this.

MR TULLIVER (*thoughtful*). So, Wakem's going to send his lad to you.

MR STELLING. Merely a passing remark . . . nothing's settled.

MRS TULLIVER. You won't make any hasty decisions, Mr Tulliver? After all, there's no hurry. Tom only returns from the 'cademy tomorrow and he'll want to enjoy the summer.

MR TULLIVER. All the more reason to get him to a proper school. He's learnt nothing at that 'cademy but how to pull potatoes and black boots.

MRS TULLIVER. Perhaps I should kill a couple of fowl, and have the aunts and uncles to dinner. You would want to hear what they have to say?

MR TULLIVER. You may kill every fowl i' the yard, if you like, Bessy, but I shall ask neither aunt nor uncle what I'm to do wi'my own lad. No. I'm decided. You shall have him, sir, if you'll take him.

MRS TULLIVER. Dear heart!

MR TULLIVER. What's good enough for Wakem, is good enough for me.

Scene Three

The following day. At Dorlcote Mill. A great crying and screaming is heard as MAGGIE *is dragged into the parlour by*

her mother, kicking and wriggling all the while. MRS
TULLIVER *tries in vain to brush her daughter's hair.*

MRS TULLIVER. Maggie, Maggie. be quiet now. Stop this at
once. It's far too wet for little girls to go riding in open gigs
in their best bonnets. You'll see Tom as soon as your father
has fetched him. Hold still now. Hold still. Don't you want
to look pretty for Tom?

MAGGIE *suddenly rushes out of her grasp and plunges her
head into a pail of water.*

*As her head goes under, we hear the strange deaf but
booming noise that she would hear. She brings her head up,
but the noise continues.*

(*Above the noise.*) Maggie, Maggie, what is to become of
you if you are so naughty? No-one will love you anymore.
Oh, look at your clean pinafore! Folks 'ull think I've done
something wicked to have such a child. It's a judgement on
me.

During this speech, MAGGIE *has run to the upper
platform, which is now her attic.*

*Lost in her deaf rage. She picks up her fetish – the trunk of
a large wooden doll and begins to beat and grind it and
hurl it against the wall, until gradually the noise subsides
and she calms. She pets the doll and kisses it better.*

Down below, BOB JAKIN *has entered, with a large barrel
of flour.* MAGGIE *sees him and runs down the steps. She
spins round and round –*

MAGGIE. Tom's coming home. Tom's coming home. Bob,
Tom's coming home today.

BOB. I know that.

MAGGIE. Can I come into the Mill?

BOB. No, you can't.

MAGGIE. Why?

BOB. Because if the maister saw me dallyin' with you instead
'o doin' my work, he'd whip me good an' proper like he did
for not frightenin' the birds.

MAGGIE. Bob? How old are you?

BOB. Thirteen.

MAGGIE. I'm nine.

BOB. I know that.

MAGGIE. Can you read?

BOB. No. I'm no reader, I aren't.

MAGGIE. Do you want me to teach you?

BOB. No thank you, if it's all the same to you.

MAGGIE. But don't you want to know things? There are countries full of creatures called elephants and civet cats and sun-fish, instead of horses and cows, you know. Don't you want to read about them?

BOB. I'll go an' see 'em wi' me own eyes, I will. I'm going to work on the ships and see the whole world as soon as I's growed enough.

MAGGIE. So am I. But I'll read about things first.

BOB. Tell your brother there's a rattin' tonight. He can come with me. I know the chap as owns the ferrets. He's the biggest rot-catcher anywhere, he is. I'd sooner be a rot-catcher nor anything, I would.

MAGGIE. I thought you wanted to work on the ships.

BOB. I'm goin' to do both, I am. I'm goin' to hev white ferrets wi' pink eyes and catch my own rots, an put a rot in a cage wi' a ferret, an' see 'em fight.

MAGGIE. That's cruel.

BOB. So? It's only rots.

MAGGIE. What if the rot . . . rat you catch has babies, waiting for it to come home?

BOB. All the better.

MAGGIE. But they're our fellow creatures, Bob. We ought to care about them.

BOB. You can talk. You'll catch it from your brother when he sees his rebbits are all dead.

MAGGIE. Dead? (*Tremulously.*) What? The lop-eared one and the spotted doe?

BOB. As dead as moles.

MAGGIE (*bursting into tears*). But Tom told us to take care of them.

BOB. Told you.

MAGGIE. He told me to be sure and remember them every day but how could I when they didn't come into my head? He'll be so angry. What am I going to do? What am I going to do?

BOB. You could hide, miss. That's what I'd do. (*He goes.*)

MAGGIE *begins to panic. She takes large gasping breaths. She runs about the yard in desperation.*

MAGGIE. Oh, it's cruel, it's cruel. Oh please don't let the rabbits be dead. No. No. No. Oh please let them be very well and make me have fed them and make Tom be pleased with me. Oh please, please.

Music. TOM *is born in aloft on his father's shoulders, wearing a laurel wreath. He is surrounded by a cheering crowd. He leaps down and goes straight to* MAGGIE *and clasps her in his arms as if she is the most precious thing in his life.* MAGGIE *is thrilled.*

The music stops. The crowd goes. TOM, *just a boy now, is standing before* MAGGIE.

TOM. Hello, Maggie.

MAGGIE (*hurling herself around his neck and kissing him*). Tom, Tom . . . (TOM *allows this but keeps his arms by his side.*) Mother wouldn't let me go to meet you. But I wanted to. I really did.

TOM. What happened to your hair?

MAGGIE. I'm sick of it.

TOM *suddenly runs and jumps high to touch the branch of a tree.* MAGGIE *copies him.*

TOM. Guess what I've got in my pockets.

MAGGIE. Is it marbles?

TOM. Marbles? No. I've swopped all my marbles with the little ones.

MAGGIE. What then?

TOM. Guess.

MAGGIE. How am I supposed to guess?

TOM. Don't be a spitfire or I won't tell you.

MAGGIE. Oh please tell me. I won't be a spitfire Tom, I
promise. Please.

TOM. All right. It's two new fish-lines. One for me and one for
you. I wouldn't go halves on the toffee and gingerbread on
purpose to save the money and Gibson and Spouncer fought
with me because I wouldn't.

MAGGIE. Oh Tom!

TOM. We'll go fishing tomorrow at the Round Pool and you
can catch one yourself and put the worms on and everything.
(MAGGIE *throws her arms around his neck.*). Wasn't I a
good brother, now, to buy you a line all to yourself?

MAGGIE. Yes, very, very, very good. I do love you Tom.

TOM. And the boys fought with me because I wouldn't give in
about the toffee.

MAGGIE. I wish you wouldn't fight at your school. Did they
hurt you?

TOM. Of course not. I gave Spouncer a black eye. That's what
he got for wanting to leather me. Come on.

MAGGIE. Where are we going?

TOM. To look at the rabbits.

Music. A terrible sickening dread fills MAGGIE'*s heart.*

MAGGIE. Tom, how much money did you give for your
rabbits?

TOM. Two half-crowns and a sixpence.

MAGGIE. I think I've got more than that in my steel purse
upstairs. I'll ask mother to give it you.

TOM. What for? I don't need your money.

MAGGIE. To buy some more rabbits with.

TOM. Rabbits? I don't want anymore.

MAGGIE. But they're all dead.

Pause.

TOM. You forgot to feed them. And Bob Jakin forgot. I'll kill him. I'll have him turned off our land. And I don't love you, Maggie. And you won't be coming fishing with me.

MAGGIE. Tom, I couldn't help it, I forgot. I'm very, very sorry.

TOM. You're a stupid girl and I don't love you.

MAGGIE. Oh, please forgive me Tom, please. I'd forgive you if you forgot anything.

TOM. Now you just listen to me, Maggie: aren't I a good brother to you?

MAGGIE. Yes. And I do love you so much, Tom.

TOM. But you're a naughty girl. Last holidays you licked the paint off my lozenge-box and the holidays before that you pushed your head through my kite all for nothing.

MAGGIE (*beginning to hear the boom of a deaf rage*).
I couldn't help it.

TOM. Yes you could, you could if you'd minded what you were doing.

MAGGIE. I couldn't . . .

TOM. You're a naughty girl and you're not coming fishing with me. Now, go away.

MAGGIE*'s rage is now very loud. She runs to the attic and throws herself on the ground, sobbing. Down below,* BOB JAKIN *enters. Above* MAGGIE*'s rage we hear –*

TOM. You let my rabbits die.

BOB. I did not.

TOM. That's a lie.

TOM *launches into him. They fight ferociously as* MAGGIE*'s deaf rage reaches a peak.* MR TULLIVER *enters.*

MR TULLIVER. What's this? What's this? Fighting already?

He pulls them apart. BOB *runs off.*

TOM. He killed my rabbits. Him and Maggie. They killed them.

MR TULLIVER. Killed them?

TOM. I told them to feed them and they didn't.

MR TULLIVER. Well, they'd happen ha' died, if they'd been
fed. They're nesh things, them lop-eared rabbits. I told you
that. Things out o' natur never thrive. Where's your little
sister?

TOM. I don't know.

MR TULLIVER. But she was with you. You've been naughty
to her, haven't you?

TOM. No, father. I only told her about the rabbits.

MR TULLIVER. She'll be in the attic, I doubt. You go and
fetch her down and bring her for her tea. And be good to
her, d'you hear? Else I'll let you know better.

He leaves. TOM *shuffles about, trying to overcome his
absolute unwillingness to go and be nice to* MAGGIE.
Slowly, he climbs to the attic.

MAGGIE, *who has been crouching in a corner, perks up
when she hears the footsteps, and waits in trepidation, to
see who it will be.* TOM *reaches the top of the steps and
stops.*

TOM. Maggie, you're to come down for your tea.

She rushes to him and clings around his neck and sobs –

MAGGIE. Oh, Tom, Tom, please forgive me. I can't bear it,
I'm so sorry and I'll always be good and remember things, I
will. Please love me, Tom. Please. Please.

She caresses him and kisses his ears.

TOM. All right. All right. Don't cry, Magsie. Don't cry.

They cuddle and hug each other.

SceneFour

Music.

MAGGIE *and* TOM *are sitting on the upper platform, as if at
the edge of the pool, fishing. Each sits very straight and quiet*

(which is agony for MAGGIE) *with his new rod dangling in the water.*

Pause.

MAGGIE. What if there aren't any fish?

TOM. Shh. The round pool is full of fish. Everyone knows that. There was a big flood once when the round pool was made. Father told me. The animals all drowned and boats went all over the fields and everything. When I'm a man, I'll make a boat with a wooden house on the top of it, like Noah's Ark. And if a flood came, I wouldn't mind and I'd take you in.

MAGGIE. What would we eat?

TOM. Rabbits. I'd hit 'em on the head as they swam by.

Cut to: the parlour at the mill. MRS TULLIVER *is ministering to* AUNT *and* UNCLE GLEGG.

AUNT GLEGG *is sitting very straight in her chair and tapping her watch.*

MRS GLEGG. Half past five. Whatever time it might be by other people's clocks and watches, it has gone half-past five by mine.

MRS TULLIVER. Oh dear, I'm sure Sister Pullet will be here in time, sister. The tea won't be ready till half-past six.

MRS GLEGG. I detest this nonsense of having your tea at half-past six, when you might have it at six. That was never the way in our family.

MRS TULLIVER. Why, Jane, what can I do? Mr Tulliver doesn't like his tea before seven, but I put it half an hour earlier for you.

MRS GLEGG. And where are those children of yours? Don't they come and greet their Aunt Glegg?

MRS TULLIVER. They're fishing at the round pool.

MRS GLEGG. Fishing! What kind of work is fishing for a gell? I'm sure I never went fishing.

MRS TULLIVER. I'd rather have her with her brother and sure of where she is, for she gets up to such mischief. I'm sure the child's half an idiot in some things; I send her upstairs to fetch something and she forgets what she's gone for, an' sits on the floor i' the sunshine plaiting her hair and singing like a Bedlam creatur. You've no idea the trouble I have.

MRS GLEGG. Well, that niver ran i' our family, thank God, no more nor a brown skin as makes her look like a gypsy. She's a Tulliver through and through. There's no Dodson there. Eh, Mr Glegg?

MR GLEGG. If you say so, dear.

Cut to: the round pool

MAGGIE. Tom? In my book it says they used to put women under water and if they swam they were witches and were killed and if they drowned and died they weren't witches. But that isn't right, is it?

TOM. Yes it is. Nasty old witches deserve to die.

Cut to: the parlour.

AUNT PULLET *enters, crying copiously, supported by* UNCLE PULLET.

MRS GLEGG. Now then Sophy, you're late. What's the matter with you?

MRS PULLET (*eventually*). She's gone. Died the day before yesterday, an' her legs was as thick as my body. They'd tapped her no end o' times and the water – they say you might ha' swum in it.

MRS GLEGG. Well it's a mercy she's gone then, whoever she may be.

MR PULLET. It's old Mrs Sutton o' the Twentylands.

MRS GLEGG. She's no kin o' yours, then, nor much acquaintance as I iver heared of.

MRS PULLET. She's so much acquaintance as I've seen her legs when they was like bladders.

MRS TULLIVER. Now, you sit here, dear. There.

She exits.

MRS GLEGG. Sophy, I wonder at you, fretting and injuring your health about people as don't belong to you. That was never the way in our family.

MRS TULLIVER (*entering with a large, frilly doll – Lucy*).

And look who's here to complete our little gathering.

MRS GLEGG. Ah, Lucy. And how are you? Don't you come and kiss your Aunt Glegg? Whatever is the matter now, Sophy?

MRS PULLET. I can't look at her without thinking of our poor dead sister Deane. To think she should ha' gone so young.

MRS TULLIVER. But she doesn't look a bit like her mother. I'm sure she's more like me, for sister Deane was sallow.

MRS GLEGG. But she knows how to hold her tongue like her mother did.

MRS TULLIVER. Oh yes. It's no trouble having her visit. I can sit her on a stool for hours together and not hear a peep from her. Such a pretty little thing.

MRS PULLET. I think I'm ready to take my bonnet off, Pullet. Did you see as the cap-box was put out?

He hands the box to his wife, who ceremoniously removes her bonnet while her sisters look on.

MRS TULLIVER. What a bonnet. I'll try it on later, if I may.

MRS PULLET. Pullet payed for it. He said I was to have the best bonnet at Garam Church . . .

MR PULLET. Let the next best be whose it would.

MRS PULLET (*on the verge of tears*). And to think I may never wear it twice; who knows?

Cut to: the round pool.

TOM. Look, look, Maggie. You've caught one. Oh Magsie, you little duck! You little duck!

The fish is hauled in. MAGGIE is overcome with joy. TOM gives it a hefty whack on the ground in order to kill it and hands it to MAGGIE at the very moment she notices LUCY –

MAGGIE. *Lucy!*

She throws the fish and it lands with a slap in the middle of the parlour, causing a great flurry of panic.

MR GLEGG. God bless us!

TOM and MAGGIE descend.

MAGGIE. Lucy! I didn't know you were coming today. We caught a fish.

MRS GLEGG. Heyday! (*Silence falls.*) Do little boys and gells come into a room without taking notice o' their uncles and aunts? That wasn't the way when I was a little gell.

MRS TULLIVER. Go and speak to your aunts and uncles, my dears. And don't touch Lucy, your hands aren't clean.

MAGGIE *and* TOM *sidle towards* AUNT GLEGG.

MRS GLEGG (*loudly, as if they are deaf*). Well, and how do you do? And I hope you're good children, are you?

She takes hold of their hands, very tightly and they are forced to kiss her.

Look up, Tom, look up. Put your hair behind your ears, Maggie, and keep your frock on your shoulders.

MRS PULLET. Well, my dears, you grow wonderful fast. I doubt they'll outgrow their strength, Bessy. I think the gell has too much hair. It isn't good for her health. It's that as makes her so brown, I shouldn't wonder.

MR TULLIVER *enters just in time to hear this remark.*

MR TULLIVER. There's nothing wrong with the child. She's healthy enough. There's red wheat as well as white, for that matter, and some like the dark grain best. But I've told Bessy to have the child's hair cut, so it lies smooth.

MR GLEGG. Afternoon, neighbour Tulliver.

MR TULLIVER. Afternoon to you all.

MRS TULLIVER (*quietly to* MAGGIE). Go and brush you hair – do, for shame. I told you to be back early to change, you know I did.

MR TULLIVER. I see you're all here.

MRS GLEGG. We were all invited, weren't we?

MR TULLIVER. Well, little Lucy, is your father not with you then?

MRS TULLIVER. Busy at Guest and Co., I'm afraid.

MR TULLIVER. That's a shame now, isn't it? I would have liked your father to hear what I've got to say.

MRS GLEGG. And we won't do, I suppose?

MAGGIE *beckons* TOM *to the attic. He goes.*

MR TULLIVER. You'll do well enough. And now's as good a time as any.

MRS TULLIVER. Can't it wait until after tea, dear heart?

MR TULLIVER. You wanted me to tell'em, Bessy, so I'll tell 'em and eat the better for't. I've settled to send Tom to a Mr Stelling, a parson, down at King's Lorton. Parsons make the best schoolmasters and this fellow is the sort o' man I want.

Cut to: the attic.

TOM. There's no time to play at anything before tea. (MAGGIE *takes a pair of scissors out of her pocket.*) What are they for?

She answers by seizing a handful of her hair and cutting it.

Oh no, Maggie. You'll catch it now. (*Snip.*) Oh no, you'd better not cut off any more.

MAGGIE. I don't care. Do the back. Do the back.

TOM, *giggling now, takes the scissors and snips the back. He looks at her and collapses in laughter, rolling around and clutching his stomach.*

TOM. You should see what you look like. Look at yourself in the glass. You look like the idiot we throw our nut shells to at school.

MAGGIE (*hearing the boom of a deaf rage*). I do not.

TOM. You do, you do. Idiot. You'll have to come downstairs now. Oh no . . .

MAGGIE (*stamping and pushing him*). Don't laugh at me.

TOM. Now then, spitfire. What did you cut it for, then? I'm going for my tea.

MAGGIE. Don't go, Tom, please.

TOM. Idiot.

He runs downstairs. MAGGIE's deaf rage has risen. She goes to the mirror and peers at herself and sobs and grabs her fetish and hurls it against the wall.

Cut to: the parlour.

MRS PULLET. I hear Lawyer Wakem is sending his son – the deformed boy, to a clergyman.

MR TULLIVER. The very same. Wakem's as big a scoundrel as Old Harry ever made, but he knows the length of every man's foot. Tell me who's Wakem's butcher. and I'll tell you where to get your meat.

MRS GLEGG. It 'ud be a fine deal better for some people if they let the lawyers alone.

MR GLEGG. You'll have to pay a swinging half-yearly bill. then, Tulliver?

MR TULLIVER. A cool hundred a year, that's all. But it's an investment, you know. Tom's eddication 'ull be so much capital to him. Eh, Tom?

MR GLEGG. Ay, there's something in that. 'When land is gone and money's spent, Then learning is most excellent.' but us that have got no learning had better keep our money, eh neighbour Pullet?

MRS GLEGG. Mr Glegg, I wonder at you. It's very unbecoming in a man o' your age and belongings to be making a joke when you see your own kin going headlongs to ruin.

At this moment, MAGGIE *appears in the doorway.*

MRS TULLIVER *sees her and utters a little cry.*

MR GLEGG. Heyday! What little girl's this? I don't think I know her. It must be a little gypsy child from the common.

MR TULLIVER (*laughing*). Why, she's gone and cut her hair off herself. Did you ever know such a little hussy as it is?

MR PULLET. Why, little miss, you've made yourself look very funny.

MRS GLEGG. Fie, for shame. Little gells as cut their own hair should be whipped and fed on bread and water.

MRS PULLET. She's certainly like a gypsy now. I doubt it'll stand in her way i' life to be so brown.

MRS TULLIVER. She's a naughty child, as'll break her mother's heart.

MAGGIE *begins to cry. Her father goes to her.*

MR TULLIVER. Come, come, my wench, never mind. You was i' the right to cut it off if it plagued you. Give over crying now.

MRS GLEGG. Spoiling the child like that will be the ruin of her. Just as bringin' the boy up above his fortin' will be the ruin of him.

MR TULLIVER (*flaring up*). I don't need you to tell me how to raise my own youngsters.

MAGGIE *goes to* TOM *for comfort. He pulls her hair.*

TOM. Idiot.

MAGGIE *runs out.*

MRS GLEGG. O, I say nothing. My advice has never been asked for and I don't give it.

MR TULLIVER. It'll be the first time then. It's the only thing you're over-ready at giving.

MRS GLEGG. I've been over-ready at lending, then. There's folks I've lent money to as perhaps I shall repent o' lending money to kin.

MRS TULLIVER. Sister, can I get you some almonds and raisins?

MRS GLEGG. Bessy, I'm sorry for you. It's poor work talking o' almonds and raisins.

MRS PULLET. Lors, sister Glegg, don't be so quarrelsome. It's very bad among sisters.

MRS GLEGG. Indeed it is bad, when one sister invites another to her house o' purpose to quarrel with her.

MR TULLIVER. I should never want to quarrel with any woman if she kept her place.

MRS GLEGG. My place! You wouldn't have the chance to stand there abusing me, if there hadn't been them in our family who married worse than they might ha' done.

MR TULLIVER. My family's as good as yours, and better, for it hasn't got a damned ill-tempered woman in it.

MRS GLEGG. Well. I don't know whether you think it's a fine

thing to sit by and hear me swore at, Mr Glegg, but I'm not going to stay a minute longer in this house. You may take the gig home. I will walk.

She leaves.

MR GLEGG (*following*). Dear heart, dear heart. It's almost dark.

MRS TULLIVER. Mr Tulliver, how could you talk so?

MR TULLIVER. Let her go. And the sooner the better. We'll eat our tea now, Bessy. Some of us are hungry as have done a day's work. Go and fetch your sister from the attic, Tom.

TOM *runs up the stairs, calling 'Maggie'.*

MRS TULLIVER. Sister Pullet, do you think you should go after her and try to pacify her?

MRS PULLET. I don't know what could pacify her in such a mood.

MR TULLIVER. Leave her, I say. She won't be trying to domineer over me again, in a hurry.

TOM (*returning*). She isn't there.

MRS TULLIVER. Where is she then?

MRS PULLET *bursts into tears.*

Scene Five

Somewhere on the road to the common, MAGGIE *is running. It is starting to get dark. A* MAN *enters infront of her. She sees him and stops. He looks like a gypsy. He approaches.*

MAN. Have you got a copper, to give a poor man?

MAGGIE. I haven't got any money.

MAN. What? Nothing at all?

MAGGIE. My uncle Pullet usually gives me sixpence, but he didn't this time. I've got my silver thimble. You can have that. (*She hands it to him.*)

MAN. Thank you kindly. And where are you off to, pretty lady?

MAGGIE. To the gypsies on the common. I've run away.

MAN. Have you now? That's interesting.

MAGGIE. Everyone says I'm a gypsy really. I'm going to live
with them and I think they'll make me their Queen when
they find out how much I know. I'm going to teach them
how to read. (*The* MAN *starts to laugh.*) I'm not an idiot. I
just cut my hair.

MAN. Oh no, I'm sure you're not an idiot, Your Majesty. And
you know which way to go, do you? To find the gypsies.

MAGGIE. Yes . . . well, I thought I did.

MAN. Give me your hand, then, and I'll take you to 'em. I'm
going that way myself and I'm sure they'll be very grateful
to me for bringing them their Queen. (*He holds out his hand
to her.*) Your Majesty . . . (MAGGIE *hesitates.*) Your
Majesty . . .

MAGGIE *is about to take his hand, but as she looks at him
the lights grow dark and there is a strange red glow around
him and he gradually takes the shape of the* BLACKSMITH
*who is the devil, with his leathern apron and his arms
akimbo and a great laugh. He grabs her and she screams
and doesn't stop screaming until* MR TULLIVER *has
entered and taken her in his arms and the devil has gone.*

MAGGIE (*sobbing*). Father.

MR TULLIVER. You mustn't think o' running away from
father. What 'ud father do without his little wench?

MAGGIE. Father . . . I saw the devil.

MR TULLIVER. I know, I know. But father 'll take your part,
Maggie. Always remember that. Father 'll take your part.

*He carries her back to the parlour and sits down and rocks
her.* TOM *and* MRS TULLIVER *gather round.*

She's sleeping now.

MRS TULLIVER. She must have been running for hours.

MR TULLIVER. Now you listen to me, both of you; I won't
have a single word said to her about this, d'you understand?
No teasing and no harsh words. Eh, Tom?

TOM. Yes, father.

MR TULLIVER. I want you to be good to your sister. For she feels things. And she loves you very much.

TOM. Father? You wouldn't want me to go to school with Wakem's son, would you?

MR TULLIVER. It doesn't matter much. The lad's a poor mismade creatur. Takes after his dead mother in the face. Don't you learn anything bad of him, that's all.

Scene Six

Music.

MAGGIE *and* TOM *are holding hands, staring at the river. The air is full of the sound of the water rushing through the mill wheel.*

After a moment, MAGGIE *turns to* TOM *and kisses him.*

TOM *takes his place at his desk in the schoolroom.* MAGGIE *sits cross-legged and reads her book.* MR STELLING *enters.* TOM *is gazing dreamily towards* MAGGIE.

MR STELLING. ' . . . sunt etiam volucrum . . . ' Yes? Sunt etiam volucrum . . . (*Suddenly rapping the desk with his stick.*) Tulliver.

TOM. Sir?

MR STELLING. Go on please. (TOM *cannot begin.*) This is not good enough. Not good enough at all. What are you thinking about, Tulliver?

TOM. I . . . I don't know, Sir.

MR STELLING. You feel no interest in what you are doing, Sir. Inability to understand is one thing, but plain indifference is quite another. I will not tolerate it. Now. Let us try again – Sunt etiam volucrum . . .

There are tears gathering in TOM's *eyes. He scratches the side of his face in a vain attempt to hide them.*

TOM. Sunt etiam volucrum . . . ut ostrea . . .

MR STELLING. No.

TOM. Ut . . .

MR STELLING. No. (*Losing patience.*) Sunt etiam volucrum ceu passer, hirundo . . .

TOM. Sunt etiam volucrum ceu passer hirundo. Sunt etiam volucrum ceu passer hirundo.

MR STELLING goes. TOM charges about the stage. He is angry and frustrated. He runs to the garden and picks up a stick and beats everything in sight.

PHILLIP enters and sits down with a sketchpad and pencil. He begins to draw.

TOM watches him suspiciously for several moments, until his curiosity gets the better of him and he approaches.

TOM. (*looking at* PHILLIP'*s drawings*). That's a donkey with paniers. And that's a spaniel. I wish I could draw like that. I'm going to learn drawing this half.

PHILLIP. You can do it without learning. I never learnt. You just have to look carefully at things and draw them again and again.

Pause.

TOM. I hate Latin, do you?

PHILLIP. I don't really care about it.

TOM. But have you got into the Propria quae maribus yet?

PHILLIP. I've finished all the grammar.

TOM. So you won't have the same lessons as me?

PHILLIP. No. But I'll help you, if you like. I'd be glad to.

TOM (*after taking this in*). I don't see why we have to learn Latin anyway.

PHILLIP. It's part of a gentleman's education. You can study what you like eventually and forget your Latin. That's what most people do.

TOM. That's what I'll do. But I won't study. I'll buy a horse and ride round my land like my father does.

PHILLIP. Do you like Greek history? I do. I would like to have been a Greek and fought the Persians and then have come home and written tragedies or have been listened to by

everybody for my wisdom, like Socrates, and died a grand
death.

TOM. Were the Greeks fighters? Are there stories like Attila
the Hun in the Greeks?

PHILLIP. Yes. Lots.

TOM. But are they all in greek?

PHILLIP. I've got them in english too. You can read them.

TOM. I don't like reading.

PHILLIP. I'll tell you them, then. As many as you want.

Pause.

TOM. Do you love your father?

PHILLIP (*blushing slightly*). Yes, don't you love yours?

Scene Seven

In the garden, a week later. TOM *runs in and throws himself
on the ground.* PHILLIP *enters, wielding a stick.*

TOM. Come on! What happens now?

PHILLIP. Now Odysseus takes the burning pike and thrusts it
into the Cyclops' eye.

TOM. No he doesn't.

PHILLIP. Yes he does. And the Cyclops roars with pain.

TOM. But I'm a big giant and you're just a tiny little man.

PHILLIP. Yes, but you're asleep because I've plied you with
wine.

TOM. I wouldn't have drunk it.

PHILLIP. You did drink it, and then I escape with my men
because you're blind.

TOM. No you don't.

PHILLIP. Yes I do.

TOM (*sitting up*). I don't want to do this story anymore.

PHILLIP. All right. It was you who asked for it.

Pause.

TOM (*suddenly making a grab for the stick*). Right, I'm
Odysseus now, and you're the Cyclops.

PHILLIP *topples to the ground.* TOM *goes to help him.*

PHILLIP. Get away! You big lumbering idiot.

TOM. If I'm a lumbering idiot, you're an imp – a mean little
imp and if you weren't no better than a girl, I'd hit you. And
I'm an honest man's son and your father's a rogue.
Everybody says so.

PHILLIP (*tearful*). Well you're no better than a cart-horse,
Tulliver. You're not fit to talk to a cart-horse.

He leaves. TOM *is angry and upset. Suddenly* MAGGIE *is
there.*

TOM. Maggie! How long can you stay? Till Christmas?

MAGGIE. Two weeks.

TOM. Yes!

*He grabs her round the waist and they dance round and
round until they are dizzy.* PHILLIP *is watching with
curiosity from the shadows.* MAGGIE *catches sight of him.
He goes.*

MAGGIE. There was somebody there, then.

TOM. A creature with a hump? That's Wakem; the lawyer's
son. And you're not to talk to him or go anywhere near him
because he's mean and crafty. Now mind you don't. Has my
father beaten his father yet?

MAGGIE. I don't know. But he talks a lot about it and goes
red in the face.

TOM. We'll show him.

MAGGIE (*looking about*). Look at all these books. I'd love to
have this many books.

TOM. You couldn't read one of them. They're in Latin.

MAGGIE. I can read the back of that one. 'History of the
Decline and Fall of the Roman Empire.'

TOM. Well, what does that mean? You don't know.

MAGGIE. I could soon find out.

TOM. How?

MAGGIE. I could open it. (*She picks up another.*)

TOM. You can't understand that one.

MAGGIE (*opening it and trying to read*). 'Nomen non creskens genittivo . . . '

TOM. 'Creskens genittivo! Creskens genittivo!' It's 'Crescens genitivo.'

MAGGIE. So? I could do it if I'd learnt what you'd learnt.

TOM. No you couldn't. Girls can't do Latin. 'Creskens genittivo!'

MAGGIE. I could work it out.

TOM. No you couldn't.

MR STELLING *enters.* PHILLIP *hovers behind him.*

MR STELLING. Ah. Here you both are. Impressing her with your learning, are you, Tulliver?

MAGGIE. Mr Stelling? Couldn't I do Latin and all Tom's lessons if you were to teach me?

TOM. Girls can't do Latin, can they, Sir?

MR STELLING. Well . . . They can pick up a little of everything, I daresay. They've got a great deal of superficial cleverness; but they couldn't go far into anything. They're quick and shallow. Come along now. Roast beef for dinner. Which would you rather decline, Tulliver – roast beef, or the Latin for it?

TOM (*hesitating*). Roast beef, sir.

MR STELLING (*chuckling*). Roast beef, eh? Roast beef.

He goes.

TOM. Ha, ha, Miss Maggie. It's not so good to be quick after all. Ha, ha, Miss Maggie.

MAGGIE. Shut up.

TOM. Ha, ha, Miss Maggie. Ha, ha, Miss Maggie.

She closes her ears. A deaf rage has begun. TOM *goes.*

Scene Eight

PHILLIP *stands in the middle of the schoolroom and begins to sing.* MAGGIE *gradually comes out of her rage and listens to him. She is enchanted. She moves nearer. He stops.*

MAGGIE. Don't.

PHILLIP. What?

MAGGIE. Stop.

PHILLIP. Maggie?

MAGGIE. Yes.

PHILLIP. I'm Phillip.

MAGGIE. It's beautiful.

PHILLIP. I like to sing.

MAGGIE. At Christmas, angels come and sing outside our window. Tom says it's just the Parish choir but I know it's angels.

PHILLIP. I'm sure it is. You don't look like Tulliver's sister.

MAGGIE. I'm dark. Like a . . . like my father. Do you know Latin?

PHILLIP. Yes. And Greek. You would if you were taught.

MAGGIE. Will you teach me?

PHILLIP. Won't you be going to school?

MAGGIE. I'll go to boarding school with my cousin Lucy. But we won't do Latin. I think it's sewing mostly.

PHILLIP. I'll teach you what I can. You have dark eyes. They're not like other eyes. They seem as if they are trying to speak . . .

MAGGIE. What do they say?

PHILLIP. They are trying to speak kindly. I don't like other people to look at me, but I like you to look at me.

MAGGIE. I will always look at you. I am so, so sorry for you. (PHILLIP *turns away.* MAGGIE *realises her mistake.*) But you are very clever, and you can sing like an angel. I wish you were my brother as well as Tom. You would stay at home with me when Tom went out and you would teach me everything.

PHILLIP. You'll go away soon and forget about me. And when you're grown up, you'll see me and you won't take any notice of me.

MAGGIE. I won't forget you. I never forget anything and I think about everybody when I'm away from them. (*Pause.*) Would you like me to kiss you, as I kiss Tom? I will if you like.

PHILLIP. Yes, very much: nobody kisses me.

MAGGIE *puts an arm around his neck and kisses him earnestly.*

MAGGIE. I will always remember you, and kiss you when I see you again, even if it's a very long time.

MAGGIE *glances round and finds* TOM *looking at her from the doorway. He goes. The lights dim.*

The crowd have gathered on the upper platform. They repeat some of the actions used in ducking the witch.

Scene Nine

In MAGGIE*'s room at boarding school.* LUCY *enters. (she is real now, but dressed identically to the doll).*

She combs MAGGIE*'s hair and dresses it in a grown-up style. The two girls sit together and begin to sew.*

TOM *enters. He is dressed as a man now, in tails and a stand-up collar. He looks very serious and pale.*

TOM. Maggie. Lucy.

MAGGIE. Tom. What are you doing here?

She runs and kisses him but he hardly responds.

TOM. Maggie, we're to go home immediately.

MAGGIE. What's wrong?

TOM. Father has lost the lawsuit. We are ruined.

MAGGIE. Lost . . . (LUCY *takes her arm.*)

TOM. Father is very ill. The news has . . . he has had a sort of seizure, I think.

MAGGIE. Is he . . . ?

TOM. Mother says he has been asking for you.

LUCY. I'll get your things. Shall I come with you?

TOM. No, Lucy. Thank you. I think it would be better if just Maggie and I . . . (*He is overcome.* MAGGIE *hugs him.*)

LUCY. If there's anything I can do to help, you will tell me, won't you? Anything at all.

She goes, leaving brother and sister alone.

Scene Ten

Music.

At the mill. As MAGGIE *and* TOM *enter the parlour, they see* THE BAILIFF *walking about the room, picking up objects, and examining them.*

BAILIFF. Good day to you.

TOM. Good day. (*Pause.*) Where is my mother? Mrs Tulliver?

BAILIFF. I don't rightly know. She left me here ten minutes since.

MAGGIE (*whispering to* TOM). Who is that?

TOM *begins looking for his mother.*

TOM. Mother! Mother!

MAGGIE. Who is that, Tom? That's not Doctor Turnbull.

TOM. It's the bailiff. Mother!

They hear the sound of someone sobbing and go towards it. It is coming from a wardrobe. MRS TULLIVER *is inside, sitting amongst her linen and 'chany', quite distraught.*

MRS TULLIVER. Oh my boy, my boy. To think as I should live to see this day. We're ruined. Everything is to be sold up. We shall be beggars, we must go to the workhouse. To think as your father should ha' married me to bring me to this.

MAGGIE. Mother, what's happening? Where is my father?

MRS TULLIVER. To think o' these cloths as I spun myself,
and I marked 'em so as nobody ever saw such marking –
and they're all to be sold and go into strange people's
houses and I meant 'em for you. I wanted you to have all
this pattern. Maggie could have had the large check, it never
looks good when the dishes are on it.

TOM. But surely my aunts won't let them be sold, Mother.
Haven't you sent to them?

MRS TULLIVER. Yes. Directly they put the bailies in. But I
know they'll none of them take my chany for they all found
fault with 'em when I bought 'em 'cause o' the small gold
sprig between the flowers. And I bought 'em wi' my own
money as I'd saved ever since I was turned fifteen and the
silver teapot too. (MAGGIE *begins to hear the boom of a
deaf rage.*) And I did say to him times and times, 'Whativer
you do, don't go to law'. And I've had to sit by while my
own fortin's been spent. You'll have niver a penny my boy,
but it isn't your poor mother's fault.

TOM. Don't fret, Mother. I'll get money. I'll get a situation of
some sort.

MRS TULLIVER. Bless you, my boy. I shouldn't ha' minded
so much if we could have kept the things with my name on.

MAGGIE. Stop it. How can you talk like that? As if you only
cared for things with your name on? Don't you care for my
father? Tom . . . Tom, you shouldn't let anyone find fault
with my father. Where is he? Where?

She runs to find him. TOM *and her mother follow.*

MR TULLIVER *is lying silently on a bed.* MAGGIE *falls
on her knees beside him.*

MRS TULLIVER. Dr Turnbull says it was a stroke, brought on
by the . . . the shock. He fell from his horse. They can't say
how long it may be before he recovers. Perhaps he may
never . . .

TOM. Don't, Mother.

MRS TULLIVER. But he has roused himself a couple o' times.
He's asked for you, Maggie. So there's hope, they say.

MAGGIE. Father . . . Father, it's Maggie. I'm here now. I
won't leave you. I will never leave you.

Scene Eleven

In the parlour. AUNT *and* UNCLE GLEGG, AUNT *and*
UNCLE PULLET, MRS TULLIVER, MAGGIE *and* TOM
have gathered. MRS TULLIVER, *half deranged by the*
thought of losing her possessions, is intent on laying out a tea
party on the floor.

MRS TULLIVER. Now, sister, you must sit here, and Sophy,
you must sit here and then Lucy . . . Lucy goes there . . .

TOM. Lucy isn't here, mother.

MRS TULLIVER. Not here? But there's a cup for her. Oh . . .
oh . . . well then, I shall go there and . . . no . . .

MRS GLEGG. Bankrupt. There's never been such disgrace in
the family, I'm sure.

MRS PULLET (*sobbing*). I doubt he's got the water on his
brain. It's much if he ever gets up again.

MRS GLEGG. You must bring your mind to your
circumstances, Bessy, and be thinking whether you shall get
so much as a flock bed to lie on and a stool to sit on. And if
you do, it'll be because your friends have bought 'em.
You're dependent upon us for everything now.

MRS PULLET. And if he does he'll most like be childish, as
Mr. Carr was, poor man. They fed him with a spoon as if
he'd been a babby.

MRS GLEGG. Sophy! You do talk of people's complaints till
it's quite indecent.

MRS TULLIVER. Shall I be mother? Yes, I think I will. What
a very fine pourer this tea-pot is. Very fine. Everyone always
says so.

TOM. Mother, don't worry about the tea.

MRS TULLIVER. But we're having a party, Tom. Now, who
takes sugar?

MR PULLET. Yes please.

MRS GLEGG. Heyday. I didn't come here for tea, sugar or no
sugar. If we aren't come for one to hear what the other 'ull
do to save a sister from the parish, I shall go home.

MRS PULLET. Well, I was here yesterday and looked at all

Bessy's linen and things and told her I'd buy in the spotted table cloths. But I can't take the teapot, for what would I do with two silver teapots?

MRS TULLIVER. Table-cloth. Did somebody say table-cloth? I've a great many table-cloths. This isn't my best one by any means.

MRS GLEGG. Bessy, do be quiet! What use is it talking o' table-cloths when the roof above your head is to be sold?

MRS TULLIVER. Sold?

MRS GLEGG. Yes, sold. The Mill, the land, the whole lot. Sold.

MRS TULLIVER. Now, who would like milk? I shall pass my chany jug round. What a pretty pattern, don't you think?

MRS PULLET (*sobbing*). They shall have to go to the workhouse.

MRS GLEGG. There was never any of our family in the workhouse, and never will be. We must settle on what's to become of 'em.

MR GLEGG. Well, young sir, now's the time to let us see the good of your learning – 'When land is gone and money's spent, Then learning . . . '

MRS GLEGG. Now's the time to bear the fruits of his father's disgrace and bring his mind to fare hard and to work hard. And his sister too, must make up her mind to be humble and work.

MRS PULLET. They'll be no servants to wait on her anymore.

TOM (*seeing* MAGGIE *is about to speak*). Be quiet, Maggie. Aunt, if it is a disgrace to the family that we should be sold up, and I do feel the disgrace, wouldn't it be better to prevent it altogether? If you and Aunt Pullet think of leaving any money to me and Maggie, wouldn't it be better to give it now, and save my mother from parting with her furniture?

Pause.

MR GLEGG. Ay, ay. What young man is this, then?

TOM. I could work and pay the interest you would lose.

MR GLEGG. Well done, Tom! Well done.

MRS GLEGG. Yes, Mr Glegg. It's pleasant work for you to be giving my money away, I'm sure. My money, as I've saved myself and it's to go and be squandered on them as have had the same chance as me, only they've been wicked and wasteful.

MAGGIE *is going into a deaf rage.*

MRS PULLET. La, Jane, how fiery you are. I'm sure you'll have the blood in your head and have to be cupped.

MRS TULLIVER (*offering tea*) This one is yours, and this one is yours and . . . Oh dear, I'm getting muddled . . . and . . .

TOM. Mother . . .

MRS GLEGG. Take it away. You're a disgrace making tea when . . . it's a disgrace . . . Disgraceful.

MAGGIE. Why do you come here, then? Interfering and shouting and . . . Keep away from us and don't come finding fault with my father. He's better than any of you, he's kind. Tom and I don't ever want to have any of your money. We'd rather not have it. We'll do without you.

Pause. MRS TULLIVER *sits down abruptly.* TOM *looks angry.*

MRS GLEGG. I've said over and over again – years ago I've said – 'Mark my words, that child 'ull come to no good: there isn't a bit of our family in her.'

Scene Twelve

The following day. MAGGIE *is in the parlour.* TOM *enters, looking thoroughly miserable. He ignores* MAGGIE.

MAGGIE. Did you speak to Uncle Deane? Will he find you a situation?

TOM. I don't know.

MAGGIE. But did he speak kindly?

TOM. I don't care about him speaking kindly, I just want a job. All that wasted time with Latin and . . . he says I've had all the rough work taken out of me. He makes out I'm good for nothing. He doesn't even seem to think I'm fit to work on a wharf or in a warehouse. But I am. I'll do it. He says I must learn book-keeping and calculation.

MAGGIE. If only I was Lucy Bertram in Walter Scott's novel. She was taught book-keeping by double entry, after the Italian method. Then I could teach you.

TOM. Teach. Yes. You teach, that's always the tone you take.

MAGGIE. I was only joking, Tom.

TOM. But it's always the same. You're always setting yourself up above me and everyone else. You shouldn't have spoken to my aunts like that. You shouldn't speak to anyone like that. You should leave it to me to take care of my mother and you and not put yourself forward. I can judge things better than you. It's time you started to learn that.

MAGGIE (*fighting a deaf rage*). I don't put myself above you. You often think I'm being conceited when I don't mean to be. I know you behave better than me. I know. But I don't see why you have to be so harsh.

TOM. I'm always kind to you and I always will be but you must listen to what I say and act on it.

Music.

MAGGIE *runs to the attic. She is sobbing and the rage is booming in her ears. Gradually, she calms and goes to the mirror. She looks at herself, trying perhaps, to see herself the way others see her. She feels the weight of* TOM's *words and knows she will have to change. Life isn't how she thought it was. She was wrong.*

Gradually a new MAGGIE *looks back at her – a more subdued, introspective* MAGGIE, *with her hair tied back, who steps out from the mirror and takes the* FIRST MAGGIE *in her arms and comforts her.*

SECOND MAGGIE. Don't look for love, Maggie. There is no love in life, and no happiness.

They cry together.

Scene Thirteen

Music.

SECOND MAGGIE, TOM, *and* MRS TULLIVER *huddle round* MR TULLIVER*'s sick bed. The bailiff begins to auction the furniture and all* MRS TULLIVER*'s household goods. Each item is named and followed by a cry of 'sold', at which the Tullivers shudder. Then the item is placed at the back of the stage. As more items are sold the cry of 'sold' becomes louder and the shudder more pronounced. Eventually, all that is left in the parlour is the family Bible. A large dust sheet is thrown over everything at the back.*

Scene Fourteen

MR WAKEM *is standing in the parlour, looking about with interest.* MRS TULLIVER *enters. She is shaky and a little confused.*

MRS TULLIVER. Yes? Can I help you? The sale is over . . . quite over. Yes, over, as you can tell, and I don't see how you can have any right now to be standing with your boots on in . . . .

WAKEM. My parlour? My name is Wakem. I'm the new owner of the mill.

MRS TULLIVER. You have . . . bought . . .

WAKEM. You must be Mrs Tulliver.

MRS TULLIVER. Yes. I'm . . . perhaps you remember me – Miss Elizabeth Dodson as was . . . Father was close friends with Squire Darleigh, and we allays went to the dances there – the Miss Dodsons. Perhaps you remember . . . perhaps we danced . . .

WAKEM. I believe your husband is still poorly, madam.

MRS TULLIVER. Yes, sir.

WAKEM. Should he recover his health, I think it only fair that I offer him the position of manager. That way you and your family may stay on here. He must be made to understand, however, that he would be answerable to me. I will wait two weeks for your answer. I trust that appears reasonable. Good day.

MRS TULLIVER. Reasonable . . . yes, thank you . . . .

He leaves. MRS TULLIVER *leaves.*

TOM *enters, shortly followed by* MAGGIE. *The empty room is appalling. They are silent for several moments, just looking at the places where things once stood.*

MAGGIE. Is this all? Where are the books? There's only your old school books here. I thought Uncle Glegg was going to buy the books.

TOM. Don't start, Maggie . . .

MAGGIE. I won't. (*With strange resignation.*) I won't.

Scene Fifteen

TOM *and* MAGGIE *help* MR TULLIVER *into the parlour. He is still very weak. He looks about him at the emptiness.* MRS TULLIVER *cannot look at him, so strong is her anger.*

MR TULLIVER. Ah . . . they've sold me up then . . . they've sold me up. Am I a bankrupt? I see. (*Silence.*) I see now.

MRS TULLIVER *starts to cry.*

MR TULLIVER. Poor Bessy. Don't bear me any ill will . . . we promised one another for better or worse.

MRS TULLIVER. But I never thought it'ud be as worse as this.

TOM. Don't mother.

MRS TULLIVER. No, that's right; tell me not to speak . . . that's been the way all my life.

MR TULLIVER. Let her be. What do you mean, Bessy?

MRS TULLIVER. It's all Wakem's. He says you may stay here and manage the business and have thirty shillings a week and a horse to ride to market.

Pause.

MR TULLIVER. It's all Wakem's then? This world's too many for me.

MRS TULLIVER. I want to stay here.

TOM. Father, I don't think you should submit to be under Wakem. My uncle Deane has found me a situation – I'll get a pound a week and you can do something else when you're well.

Pause.

MR TULLIVER. Fetch the old Bible. And a pen. (TOM *and* MAGGIE *obey.*) You've got a right to say as I've brought you into trouble, Bessy. But there'll be the same grave made for us and we mustn't be bearing one another any ill will.

TOM. What am I to write, Father?

MR TULLIVER. Write as your father, Edward Tulliver, took service under John Wakem, the man as had ruined him, because I wanted to make my wife what amends I could and I wanted to die in the old place . . .

TOM. No, Father . . .

MR TULLIVER. But then write as I don't forgive Wakem, and for all I'll serve him honest, I wish evil may befall him. I wish he might be punished with shame till his own son 'ud like to forget him. Then write as you'll remember what Wakem's done to your father and you'll make him and his feel it, if ever the day comes. Make 'em feel it. And sign your name, Thomas Tulliver.

MAGGIE. Father, you shouldn't make Tom write that.

TOM. Be quiet, Maggie. I shall write it.

Scene Sixteen

Music. MAGGIE *is sitting outside the mill. It is a beautiful summer's day. The birds are singing, the water rushing. She is trying to learn Latin from one of* TOM*'s old school books, but* *her heart isn't in it. She is deeply sad. She gazes out at the fields.* FIRST MAGGIE *appears, dressed as she was when a child, with her gypsy's hair. She runs and jumps. She takes* MAGGIE*'s book from her and makes it a butterfly.* MAGGIE *smiles but then takes the book back again and goes on with the grammar.* FIRST MAGGIE *goes.*

BOB JAKIN *enters. He is wearing an oil-skin cap and a plush blue waistcoat and carries a pack. He stops infront of her.*

BOB. Sarvant, Miss Maggie.

MAGGIE. Bob. Bob Jakin.

BOB. Ay, ay, Bob Jakin it must be if there was so many Bob's as let you loose i' the mill and showed you where the spiders lived.

MAGGIE. How well you look. Will you come in?

BOB. No thank you, Miss. I'll not stop long.

TOM *arrives home from work.*

MAGGIE. Tom, look. It's Bob Jakin.

BOB. Mr Tom.

TOM (*unsmilingly*). Hello Bob. What can I do for you?

BOB. Why, nothing, Mr Tom. I've had a bit o' luck lately; I doused a fire at Torry's mill and a genleman came and told me I was a sperrited chap – but I knowed that – but then he gen me ten sovreigns an' that war summat new. Look . . . (*He takes a bag from his pocket.*) There's nine left and I'd like for you to have 'em. They mayn't go fur, but they'll help – if it's true the master's broke.

Pause. MAGGIE *is close to tears.*

TOM. I can't take them. I would be taking your fortune, and they wouldn't do me much good either.

BOB. Wouldn't they? Don't say so 'cause you think I want 'em. I aren't a poor chap.

TOM. No. I don't want to take anything from anybody. But don't think I feel your kindness less because I say no. Let me shake hands with you. (*They do so.*)

BOB. I'll keep 'em then. But you will have summat, now.

(He produces a pile of books bound with string.) I bought
these for you, Miss, special-like. They're cram-full o' print.
And there's one or two wi' pictures. You will take them,
won't you? For they're a weight to carry.

MAGGIE *(taking them)*. I never knew you were so good, Bob.
I don't think anyone ever did such a kind thing for me
before.

BOB. I can't believe that, Miss. Well, I shall be off.

TOM. Yes. Thank you again, Bob.

BOB. Be seeing you. *(He goes.)*

Pause. MAGGIE *recovers herself.*

MAGGIE. He seems happy.

TOM. Yes. He does.

MAGGIE. How were things at the wharf today?

TOM. All right.

He leaves. MAGGIE *puts the books down and sits with her
head in her hands.*

FIRST MAGGIE *appears and runs to the books.*

FIRST MAGGIE. Are there any with stories in? *(No reply.)*
Are there any with stories in?

SECOND MAGGIE. I don't want stories.

FIRST MAGGIE. This one's full of hymns.

SECOND MAGGIE. I want to know why.

FIRST MAGGIE. Why what?

SECOND MAGGIE. Why this? This awful . . . miserable,
hopeless life. What I would give to change places with Bob,
even for a day! Just to walk about and smile and love the
world as I used to. I can't bear this. I can't bear it.

FIRST MAGGIE. We could go. We could dress up as a boy
and work on the barges.

SECOND MAGGIE. Don't . . .

FIRST MAGGIE. We could run away.

SECOND MAGGIE. To the gypsies?

FIRST MAGGIE. We could go and find a great man – Walter Scott. We could tell him how miserable we are and show him how well we can read and how much Latin we've learnt . . .

SECOND MAGGIE. Be quiet.

FIRST MAGGIE. And he'd understand that we're special and do something for us . . .

SECOND MAGGIE. I said, be quiet.

FIRST MAGGIE. Why should we be good all the time? It's Mother and Father's fault. They don't know anything and they don't want to know. And Tom's the worst of all, he tries to make us feel stupid all the time but he's the one who's stupid, he's . . .

SECOND MAGGIE. Shut up, shut up, shut up. (*She puts her hand over* FIRST MAGGIE's *mouth.*) Such wicked thoughts. What kind of demon is inside me, to have such thoughts?

Pause.

FIRST MAGGIE. Are there any with stories in?

SECOND MAGGIE (*taking up the books*). 'Economy of Human Life.' 'Gregory's Letters.' 'The Imitation of Christ' by Thomas à Kempis. I've heard that name. He was a monk, I think.

FIRST MAGGIE. Let's see. (*She opens it.*) Someone's put marks at the edge of the pages. 'Know that love of thyself doth hurt thee more than anything in the world . . . if thou seekest to enjoy thy own will and pleasure, thou shalt never be quiet or free from care: for in everything somewhat will be wanting and in every place there will be some that will cross thee . . .

Music. MAGGIE *feels a strange thrill of awe.*

Thou oughtest therefore to call to mind the more heavy sufferings of others, that thou mayest the easier bear thy little adversities.'

SECOND MAGGIE. Read that again.

FIRST MAGGIE. 'Thou oughtest therefore . . . '

SECOND MAGGIE. No. The first part.

FIRST MAGGIE. 'Know that love of thyself doth hurt thee
more than anything in the world . . . '

SECOND MAGGIE. Give it to me. (*She takes it and turns the
page.*) 'I have often said unto thee, and now again I say the
same, Forsake thyself, resign thyself, and thou shalt enjoy
much inward peace and tranquility. Then shall all vain
imaginations, evil perturbations . . . evil perturbations and
superfluous cares fly away; then shall immoderate fear leave
thee, and inordinate love shall die.'

A great light fills the stage and MAGGIE *falls on her knees.*

Thank you . . . thank you.

FIRST MAGGIE *looks into the light and sees the figure of
Thomas à Kempis.*

Scene Seventeen

In the mill. MAGGIE *is on her knees, scrubbing the floor. As
she works, she sings a hymn.*

TOM *enters.*

TOM. Maggie. (*She doesn't stop.*) Maggie. You went to the
drapers in St Oggs. You asked for plain sewing work.

MAGGIE. Yes.

TOM. I don't want my sister doing such things. If you have to
do some sewing, ask about amongst our aunts. Don't go
into St Oggs parading our situation to the world.

MAGGIE. I do it to help pay the debts.

TOM. I'm aware of that.

MAGGIE. I see how hard you work, how you save. I wanted
there to be more money in the tin box when Father counted it.

TOM. Listen to me: I'll take care the debts are paid. There's no
need for you to lower youself.

MAGGIE. But . . . I'm sorry, Tom. I didn't realise it would make you angry. (*She begins to scrub again.*)

TOM. Mother tells me you have started sleeping on the floor.

MAGGIE. When I feel I deserve to.

TOM. Deserve to?

MAGGIE. For a penance.

TOM. This is so typical of you. It's excessive. I want it to stop. I want you to start going out and . . .

MAGGIE. I do go out.

TOM. Yes, you walk in the Red Deeps where no-one sees you. We are not so poor that . . .

MAGGIE. It has nothing to do with our poverty. It has to do with my soul, something you would not . . .

TOM. What?

MAGGIE. Forgive me, Tom. I will obtain the sewing more quietly in future.

There is the sound of voices in the yard. TOM *looks to see who it is.*

TOM. Wakem. There's someone with him.

He leaves. MAGGIE *goes to the window and looks out. She sees a man in the yard. He looks towards her. She immediately recognizes* PHILLIP. *He raises his hat to her. She darts away from the window.*

MAGGIE. Phillip!

Music. FIRST MAGGIE *enters.*

FIRST MAGGIE. My Phillip?

She runs to the window and looks out. She waves to PHILLIP. SECOND MAGGIE *pulls her away.*

FIRST MAGGIE. I want to see him. I've missed him. He can tell me all about the world like he used to do. (*She goes to the mirror.*) 'You have dark eyes . . . '

SECOND MAGGIE (*turning the mirror to the wall*) Don't.

Scene Eighteen

MAGGIE *is walking in the Red Deeps.* PHILLIP *appears. He raises his hat, then holds out his hand to her. She takes it.*

MAGGIE. You startled me. I never meet anyone here.

PHILLIP. Forgive me. I needed to see you. I've been watching your house for days to see if you would come out. I followed you.

MAGGIE. I'm glad. I wished very much to have an opportunity of speaking to you. Shall we walk?

They do so. It is as if they are in a dream.

I like the light here. And the Scotch Firs. It is so different from the other scenery about.

PHILLIP. Yes. I remember coming here once, as a child.

MAGGIE. I was frightened to come. The Red Deeps . . .
I thought all kinds of devils and wild beasts lurked here. (*Pause.*) I have often thought of you.

PHILLIP. Not so often as I have thought of you.

MAGGIE. I wasn't sure you would remember me.

PHILLIP *takes a miniature case from his pocket and hands it to her.*

PHILLIP. It's a picture I painted of you on the last day of your visit. In the study . . .

MAGGIE. I remember my hair like that, and that pink frock. I really was like a gypsy. I suppose I still am. Am I how you expected me to be?

PHILLIP. No. You are very much more beautiful.

Pause.

MAGGIE. Phillip, you must go now and we must not see each other again. I wish we could be friends . . . I wish it could have been good and right for us, but it is not. I have lost everything I loved when I was little; the old books went, and Tom is different and my father – it is like death. But that is how it must be. I wanted you to know that if I behave as if I had forgotten you, it is not out of pride or – any bad feeling.

PHILLIP. I know what there is to keep us apart, Maggie.

I would always want to obey my father but I will not,
cannot obey a wish of his that I do not feel to be right.

MAGGIE. I don't know . . . I have sometimes thought that I
shouldn't have to give up anything and I've gone on
thinking that until it seems I have no duty at all. But that is
an evil state of mind. I would rather do without anything
than make my father's life harder. He is not at all happy.

PHILLIP. Neither am I. I am not happy.

MAGGIE. I am very sorry that you say that. I have a guide
now, Phillip – Thomas à Kempis. Perhaps you have read
him. His words are the only ones that make sense to me. I
have been so much happier since I gave up thinking about
what is easy and pleasant and being discontented because I
couldn't have my own way. Our life is determined for us
and it makes the mind very free when we give up wishing
and only think of bearing what is laid upon us.

PHILLIP. For goodness sake, Maggie. I can't give up wishing.
How can we give up wishing and longing while we are
thoroughly alive? (*Pause.*) I'm sorry. I have no friend . . .
no one who cares enough about me. If I could only see you
now and then and you would let me talk to you and show
me that you cared for me and that we may always be friends
in our hearts – then I might come to be glad of my life.

MAGGIE. Oh, Phillip . . .

PHILLIP. If there is enmity between those who belong to us
we ought to try to mend it with our friendship. You must see
that.

Pause.

MAGGIE. I can't say either yes or no. I must wait and seek for
guidance.

PHILLIP. Let me see you here once more. If you can't tell me
when, I will come as often as I can until I do see you.

MAGGIE. Do so, then. (*Pause. They smile.*) How were you so
sure that I would be the same Maggie?

PHILLIP. I never doubted you would be the same. I don't
know why I was so sure; I think there must be stores laid
up in our natures that our understandings can make no

inventory of. It's like music; there are certain strains which change my whole attitude of mind. If the effect would last I might be capable of heroisms.

MAGGIE. I know what you mean – or at least, I used to. I never hear music now except the organ at church.

PHILLIP. You can have very little that is beautiful in your life. (*Taking a book from his pocket.*) Have this. I've finished with it.

MAGGIE. I've given up books. Except Thomas à Kempis and The Christian Year and the Bible. (*He offers it again.*) Don't, Phillip.

She walks on quickly.

PHILLIP. Maggie, don't go without saying good-bye. I can't go on any farther, I think.

MAGGIE. Of course. Good-bye. What a beautiful thing it seems that God made your heart so that you could care about a strange little girl you only knew for a few weeks. I think you cared more for me than Tom did.

PHILLIP. You would never love me so well as you love your brother.

MAGGIE. Perhaps not . . . but then, the first thing I remember in my life is standing with Tom by the side of the Floss, while he held my hand; everything before that is dark to me.

PHILLIP. I kept that little girl in my heart for five years; didn't I earn some part in her too?

Scene Nineteen

Music. MAGGIE *is in the attic, sewing.* FIRST MAGGIE *appears and heads towards the door.*

SECOND MAGGIE. Where are you going?

FIRST MAGGIE. To the Red Deeps.

SECOND MAGGIE. We can't go.

FIRST MAGGIE. Phillip will be waiting. It's five days now.

We should be good to Phillip and make him happy. He was always good to us.

SECOND MAGGIE. No.

She starts sewing again. FIRST MAGGIE *sits beside her. Then she moves to the door again.*

Where are you going?

FIRST MAGGIE. To the Red Deeps.

SECOND MAGGIE. We can't go.

FIRST MAGGIE. But what harm would it do? No-one would know.

SECOND MAGGIE. It would mean concealment.

FIRST MAGGIE. But . . .

SECOND MAGGIE. No. (*She starts sewing.* FIRST MAGGIE *goes to the door.*) Where are you going?

FIRST MAGGIE. To the Red Deeps. (*She holds out her hand.*)

SECOND MAGGIE (*with sudden resolution*). Very well.

They go. PHILLIP *is there. His face lights up when he sees her.*

PHILLIP. Maggie . . .

MAGGIE. This is the last time, Phillip. I don't like to conceal anything from my family. I won't do it. I know their feelings are wrong and unchristian but it makes no difference. We must part.

Pause.

PHILLIP. Then stay with me for a while and let us talk together. Will you take my hand? (*She does so. They walk.*)

PHILLIP. I have begun another painting of you. In oils, this time. You will look like a spirit creeping from one of the fir-trees.

MAGGIE. Phillip, did you mean it when you said you are unhappy and that your life means nothing to you?

PHILLIP. Yes.

MAGGIE. But why? You have so much . . . your painting, your music, your books. You can travel . . .

PHILLIP. Oh yes, I have a great number of interests. I flit from one to the other at will. I daresay that would be enough for me if I were like other men. But I am not, am I? The society at St Oggs sickens me. I am sure it is sickened by me. My life sickens me.

MAGGIE. I understand what you mean. Sometimes it seems to me that life is very hard and unbearable. But Phillip, I think we are only like children, and someone who is wiser is taking care of us.

PHILLIP. Ah yes. You have your guide to show you the way.

MAGGIE. Yes I do. Are you mocking me, Phillip?

PHILLIP. No. I only wonder how long you can go on with this.

MAGGIE. I have found great peace this last year – even joy in subduing my will.

PHILLIP. No you haven't.

MAGGIE. I have resigned myself. I bear everything . . .

PHILLIP. You are not resigned. You are only trying to stupefy yourself. It is stupefaction to shut up all the avenues by which you might engage in life.

MAGGIE. I don't want to engage in life.

PHILLIP. You were so full of life when you were a child. I thought you would be a brilliant woman – all wit and imagination. And it flashes out in your face still – there! But then you draw that veil across.

MAGGIE. Why do you speak so bitterly to me?

PHILLIP. Because I care. I can't bear to see you go on with this self-torture.

MAGGIE. I will have strength given me.

PHILLIP. No-one is given strength to do what is unnatural. You will be thrown into the world someday and then all your needs will assault you like a savage appetite.

MAGGIE. How dare you shake me in this way? You are a tempter.

PHILLIP. No, I am not. But love gives insight, Maggie.

Pause. MAGGIE *is confused and shocked.*

Do you really want to get up every day for the rest of your

life and have no company but that of your parents, nothing
to do but to read your Bible? Day after day. Think about
it. (*Pause.*) I suppose you will never agree to see me now.
(*Pause.*) What if I came to walk here sometimes, and met
you by chance? You would not have agreed to meet me.
There would be no concealment in that.

*She looks at him. There is some relief in her eyes, but she
says nothing.* PHILLIP *goes, feeling he has cause for hope.*

*The crowd have gathered above. They repeat some of the
gestures used in testing the witch.*

MAGGIE *falls to her knees, and begins to pray.* FIRST
MAGGIE *enters and tries to interrupt her prayer.* SECOND
MAGGIE *moves away and keeps praying.* FIRST MAGGIE
follows her – SECOND MAGGIE *moves. This goes on for
some time until she cannot go on with her prayer. She turns
to* FIRST MAGGIE *and embraces her.*

SECOND MAGGIE. Go then.

FIRST MAGGIE *runs to* PHILLIP *who is waiting in the red
deeps. She throws her arms around him. They laugh.*

PHILLIP. Maggie, you promised you would kiss me when you
met me again. Do you remember? You haven't kept your
promise yet.

She kisses him. It is the same simple, childish kiss. PHILLIP
looks lovingly at SECOND MAGGIE, *as he and* FIRST
MAGGIE *walk away together, hand in hand. Music.*

AUNT PULLET *steps out of the crowd above and slowly
begins to descend.*

MRS PULLET. Do you know who Lucy was standing next to
in church today? Do you know? That poor bent boy –
Lawyer Wakem's son. Dear, dear! To think o' the property
he's like to have. Phillip, I think his name is – Phillip
Wakem. And they say he's very strange and lonely, poor
Phillip. I doubt he's going out of his mind, for we never
come along the road but he's a-scrambling out o' the trees at
the Red Deeps.

MAGGIE *has blushed deeply. She looks up at* TOM *and
finds his eyes upon her.*

Scene Twenty

In the Red Deeps. PHILLIP *is singing,* MAGGIE *listens. He finishes.*

PHILLIP. I have made you sad.

MAGGIE. It's so beautiful.

PHILLIP. You inspire me. What is it, Maggie? Don't you like being the tenth Muse?

MAGGIE. Phillip, I never felt I was right in giving way about seeing you. Though this year has been so precious to me. But now the fear comes upon me strongly again that it will lead to evil.

PHILLIP. But no evil has come of it.

MAGGIE. I have started to think about the world again . . . I have impatient thoughts. I grow weary of my home and that cuts me to the heart . . .

PHILLIP. I love you, Maggie. (*Pause.*) Forgive me. Forget I ever said that.

MAGGIE. I had not thought of it.

PHILLIP. You think I am a presumptous fool.

MAGGIE. Oh, Phillip. How can you think I have such feelings? I would be grateful for any love. But . . . I had never thought of your being my lover. It seemed so far off, a dream, that I should ever have one.

PHILLIP. Do you love me?

MAGGIE. I think I could hardly love anyone better. There is nothing but what I love you for.

PHILLIP. Then my life will be filled with hope, Maggie. We do belong to each other, always?

MAGGIE. Yes. I should like us never to part. I should like to make your life very happy.

PHILLIP. I am waiting for something else – I wonder whether it will come.

She kisses him – a grown-up kiss, this time. TOM *appears from the shadows.*

TOM. Do you call this acting the part of a man and a gentleman, sir?

MAGGIE. Tom . . .

PHILLIP. What do you mean?

> FIRST MAGGIE *enters and watches in horror.*

TOM. Mean? I'll tell you what I mean. I mean taking advantage of a young girl's foolishness, daring to trifle with the respectability of a family that has an honest name to support.

PHILLIP. I deny that. I could never trifle with your sister's happiness. I honour her more than you ever could; I would give up my life for her.

TOM. Don't try your high-flown nonsense with me. Do you pretend you have any right to make professions of love to her, when neither her father nor your father would ever consent to a marriage? That's your crooked notion of honour is it?

SECOND MAGGIE. Tom, stop it . . .

PHILLIP. Is it manly of you to talk in this way to me? You are incapable of understanding what I feel for your sister. I feel so much for her that I could even desire a friendship with you.

TOM. I should be sorry to understand your feelings. You understand me: if you make the least attempt to come near her, or to keep the slightest hold on her mind, I won't be put off by your puny miserable body, I'll thrash you – I'll hold you up to public scorn. Who wouldn't laugh at the idea of your being lover to a fine girl?

> FIRST MAGGIE *has gone into a deaf rage.*

SECOND MAGGIE (*turning away*). Tom, stop it . . . stop it, please.

PHILLIP. Stay, Maggie. Let your sister speak. If she says she is bound to give me up, I shall abide by her wishes to the slightest word.

TOM. Well, Maggie? It seems you have a choice; either you swear now, solemnly, that you will have no further communication with this . . . man, or I tell my father everything. Choose.

SECOND MAGGIE. No, Tom! Please don't tell my father, he couldn't bear it.

TOM. You should have thought of that before. Choose.

SECOND MAGGIE. Phillip . . . ?

PHILLIP. It's all right, Maggie.

SECOND MAGGIE. I will do as you say.

TOM. Swear.

SECOND MAGGIE. I . . . I swear I will never meet with Phillip again without your knowledge.

TOM. Or have any communication with him.

SECOND MAGGIE. Or have any communication with him.

PHILLIP. It is enough, Maggie. It is enough. But my feelings will not change.

TOM. Come away, Maggie.

PHILLIP. I wish you to hold yourself entirely free. Trust me; believe I want only what is good for you.

TOM. Come away, Maggie.

He seizes her right wrist and pulls her. She puts out her left hand. PHILLIP *clasps it for an instant and then turns away and leaves.* FIRST MAGGIE *runs to the attic.* TOM *drags* MAGGIE *home.*

MAGGIE. Don't suppose I think you are right or that I bow to your will. I despise the way that you spoke to him. I detest your insulting allusions to his . . .

TOM. Deformity?

MAGGIE. You have been reproaching other people all your life. You are always so sure you are right. And I'll tell you why; because your mind isn't large enough to see that there is anything better than your own conduct and your own petty aims.

TOM. If your conduct is so much better, why have you needed to be deceitful? I know what I have aimed at in my conduct, and I've succeeded. I have worked, denied myself everything to pay my father's debts so that he may hold up his head before he dies. What good has your conduct brought to him or anyone else?

MAGGIE. I know I've been wrong. But I also know that I have

sometimes been wrong because I have feelings which you would be the better for. If you did anything wrong, I would be sorry for the pain it caused you. But you have always enjoyed punishing me. Even when I was a little girl you would let me go crying to bed without forgiving me. You have no pity. You have no sense of your own sins. You thank God for nothing but your own virtues. But there are feelings in this world which throw your shining virtues into darkness.

TOM. How have your precious feelings led you to serve either me or my father? By disobeying and deceiving us, by ridiculous flights into one extreme after another. I have a different way of showing my affection.

MAGGIE. Yes: because you are a man, and have power, and can do something in the world.

TOM. Then if you can do nothing, submit to those that can.

MAGGIE. I will submit to what I feel to be right. I will even submit to what is unreasonable from my father. But I will not submit to it from you.

Pause.

TOM. Very well. You need say no more to show me what a gulf there is between us. Let us remember that in future and be silent.

MAGGIE *goes to the attic.* FIRST MAGGIE *has been beating her fettish and is crying quietly now.* SECOND MAGGIE *sits down and bursts into tears. It is almost a physical pain.*

SECOND MAGGIE. Phillip . . . poor Phillip.

They cry together. SECOND MAGGIE *recovers and becomes thoughtful. She rises and walks to the mirror. Slowly, she turns it round and looks at herself. She sees that she has been mistaken. She has gained no lasting stand on serene heights above worldly temptations and conflict. She is down again in the thick of strife with her own and others' passions. There is more struggle for her and she knows she must change.*

Gradually, a new MAGGIE *looks back, a prouder, more*

worldly MAGGIE *with a coronet of black hair. She steps
from the mirror and takes the hands of her two former
selves.*

THIRD MAGGIE. Perhaps it is for the best.

Scene Twenty-One

In the parlour at the mill. MRS TULLIVER *is sewing.* MR
TULLIVER *is sitting by the fire, brooding.* TOM *is standing
nearby.* THIRD MAGGIE *enters just as he goes and sits
beside his parents.*

TOM. Father, how much money have we got in the tin-box?

MR TULLIVER. One hundred and ninety three pounds.
    You've brought less of late.

TOM. So how much more do we need to pay the creditors?

MR TULLIVER. You know how much; there's a little more
    than three hundred wanting.

TOM. And what would you say if I told you I have three
    hundred pounds in the bank?

    Pause.

MRS TULLIVER (*throwing her arms around him*). Oh, my
    boy, my boy. I knew you'd make iverything right again
    when you got a man.

MR TULLIVER. Three hundred pounds?

TOM. Yes, father. I've been sending out bits of cargo to foreign
    ports. It was Bob Jakin's idea. I borrowed the capital from
    my Uncle Glegg.

MAGGIE. Well done, Tom.

He ignores her. MR TULLIVER, *meanwhile, begins to sob.*
TOM *puts a hand on his shoulder.*

MR TULLIVER. Bessy, you must kiss me now. The lad has
    made you amends. You'll see a bit o' comfort again. (*She
    does so.*) I wish you'd brought me the money to look at,
    Tom. I should ha' felt surer.

TOM. You shall see it tomorrow, Father. I have appointed the creditors to meet at the Golden Lion in St Oggs.

MR TULLIVER. Ah, I'll get from under Wakem's thumb now, though I must leave the old place. Tom, my lad, you'll make a speech to 'em. I'll tell em' it's you as got the best part o' the money. You'll prosper in the world my lad, and if you're ever rich enough – mind this – try and get the old mill again.

TOM. I will.

MR TULLIVER. Shake hands wi' me, my lad. It's a great thing when a man can be proud as he's got a good son. I've had that luck.

TOM *does so.* MAGGIE *is desperate to show her affection but* TOM *glances coldly at her and she daren't approach him.*

Scene Twenty-Two

Music. The air is filled with the sound of water rushing through the mill wheel. MAGGIE *is on the bank, staring at the river. Her mother calls to her.*

MRS TULLIVER. Maggie. Maggie, your father's coming into the yard. I'll fetch the best glasses from upstairs. Be sure and bring the cake through.

MR TULLIVER *enters the mill-yard, at the same time as* MR WAKEM. *Both carry riding whips.*

WAKEM. Tulliver. I've just been up to the Far Close. What a fool's trick you did, spreading those hard lumps on it. I told you what would happen.

MR TULLIVER. Get somebody else to farm for you then, as 'll ask you to teach him.

WAKEM. You've been drinking, I suppose.

MR TULLIVER. I'll tell you where I've been; I've been telling my creditors I've the money to pay 'em. Telling how my son has restored the name of Tulliver. And I want no drinking to tell you as I'll serve no longer under a scoundrel.

WAKEM. Very well! You may leave my premises tomorrow. Now hold your insolent tongue and let me pass.

MR TULLIVER. I shan't let you pass. I shall tell you what I think of you first. You're too big a raskill to get hanged . . . you're . . .

WAKEM. Let me pass you insolent brute.

He attempts to push past MR TULLIVER, *who raises his whip and rushes at him. He grabs* WAKEM *by the arm and, twisting it, pulls him to the ground and begins to flog him. Wakem cries out.*

MAGGIE *has, in slow motion, begun to register what is happening. She rushes to her father.*

MAGGIE. No . . .

She takes hold of his whipping arm. He continues to bring the whip down. She takes hold of the end of the whip, but still he continues, sending her reeling across the stage with every lash. She manages to fight her way towards him. Suddenly the strength drains from him and he collapses into her arms.

MRS TULLIVER *runs on.*

WAKEM. Help me to my horse. He's broken my damned arm. You'll suffer for this, sir. Your daughter is a witness to this assault.

MR TULLIVER. Go and show your back and tell 'em I thrashed you. I've made things a bit more even i' the world. Go.

MRS TULLIVER *helps* WAKEM *off.* MR TULLIVER *collapses further.*

MAGGIE. Father . . . We must get you inside. (*Calling.*) Help us!

MR TULLIVER. Leave me . . . leave me be. I shan't get up again.

MRS TULLIVER *runs to them, shortly followed by* TOM.

MR TULLIVER. Tom, this world's been too many for me . . . But you've done what you could to make things even. Look after your mother . . . and the little wench. Kiss me Maggie . . . don't you fret, my wench . . . there'll come somebody as'll love you and take your part. Come Bessy . . . I had my turn – I beat him.

MAGGIE. But, Father . . . you forgive him . . . you forgive
    everyone now, don't you?

MR TULLIVER. No, my wench. I don't forgive him. What's
    forgiving to do? I can't love a raskill . . .

He dies.

MAGGIE. Father.

Music. FIRST *and* SECOND MAGGIE*s enter.* SECOND
MAGGIE *helps her father to his feet. He takes* FIRST
MAGGIE *in his arms and they leave.* MRS TULLIVER *and*
TOM *follow, leaving* THIRD MAGGIE *alone in her grief.*

Scene Twenty-Three

At Uncle Deane's house.

Music. LUCY *is standing in the drawing room. It is a
summer's day and the room is full of sunshine which streams
in through the open french windows.*

*She is arranging a vase of flowers, which stands on a piano,
and singing quietly.* MAGGIE *enters, carrying a case. She
smiles when she sees* LUCY *and steals up behind her.*

MAGGIE. Lucy.

LUCY. Maggie! Maggie, what are you doing here?

MAGGIE. I took an earlier coach.

LUCY. But how did you get from the turnpike?

MAGGIE. I walked.

LUCY. It's such a long way.

MAGGIE. It's no distance at all. Not for my long legs. And
    anyway, I wanted to gaze about at all the familiar hills.

LUCY. But Aunty and I had it all planned: she was going to ride
    in the carriage and I was going to trot along behind on my
    new pony. It was going to be a splendid welcoming party.

MAGGIE. I'm very glad I avoided it then. I'd far rather creep
    in by the back door.

LUCY. Now then, Miss Tulliver, stand farther away so I can inspect you properly.

MAGGIE. There's not much to see.

LUCY. What witchery is it in you, that makes you look best in shabby clothes? If I wore such a thing, no-one would notice me.

MAGGIE. This happens to be my best frock.

LUCY. Well, you must have a new one, though it suits you so well. It's the charity ball in two weeks time.

MAGGIE. I haven't any money for new dresses. I want to get a better situation so I'm saving up for more lessons.

LUCY. Now, Maggie. Are you really going to seek another situation?

MAGGIE. Yes.

LUCY. You look sad now, just speaking of it.

MAGGIE. Don't mind me. I've been in my cage too long. Being unhappy can become a bad habit.

LUCY. Well, in that case I must put you under a regime of pleasure. There will be absolutely nothing sad or dull in the whole of your visit. I mean to fill your room with all my favourite prints and the loveliest flowers from the garden.

MAGGIE. Oh Lucy. (*She hugs her.*) I really think you enjoy other people's happiness more than your own.

LUCY. It's easy for me to be happy.

MAGGIE. I often get angry at the sight of happy people and then I hate myself for it.

LUCY. What nonsense.

MAGGIE. I think I get worse as I get older. More selfish.

LUCY. I don't believe a word of it. You must banish all such gloomy thoughts. We're having a party tomorrow, for you and Aunty and Tom.

MAGGIE. Have you seen Tom?

LUCY. He used to visit a lot but he's been quite a stranger of late.

MAGGIE. I write to him at Bob's but he seldom replies.

The doorbell rings.

LUCY. I hope this is who I think it is.

MAGGIE. And who would that be, I wonder?

LUCY. Wait and see. (*Taking her hands and kissing her.*)
Maggie.

MAGGIE. Run along now, or you'll have me in tears.

LUCY *goes.* MAGGIE *tries to recover herself. Memories
flooding back and* LUCY*'s kindness to her have brought on
a rush of tears. She goes to the windows and looks out.*

Music. STEPHEN *enters. He watches her for a moment.
She turns and sees him. Their gazes lock.*

STEPHEN. Excuse me. I didn't realise there was anyone in
here . . . Miss Deane . . .

MAGGIE. I am Maggie Tulliver. Lucy's cousin.

STEPHEN. Are you now? Stephen Guest. How do you do?

MAGGIE. Very well, thank you.

STEPHEN. But surely you can't be Miss Tulliver . . .

MAGGIE. I assure you, I am. Or I was when I last looked.

LUCY (*who has entered and is standing in the doorway,
laughing*). Now then, Stephen; how does it feel to be on the
end of a laugh for once?

STEPHEN. I see. Lucy, you really are . . .

LUCY. What?

STEPHEN. Forgive me, Miss Tulliver. This designing cousin
of yours quite deceived me. She told me you had light hair
and blue eyes.

LUCY. Not at all – it was you who said so. He thought you
would be a smaller version of your mother.

STEPHEN. I wish I could always be so mistaken, and find
reality so much more beautiful than my preconceptions.

MAGGIE. Now you have proved yourself equal to the
occasion, Mr Guest, and said what you feel you ought to
say under the circumstances.

STEPHEN. I hope you will allow that even phrases of compliment have their turn to be true. A man is occasionally grateful when he says 'Thank you'.

MAGGIE. I hope you will allow that compliments are nothing but expressions of indifference.

LUCY. Dear Maggie, you always claim you are too fond of feeling admired.

MAGGIE. I am. But compliments will never make me feel so.

STEPHEN. I will never pay you a compliment again, Miss Tulliver.

MAGGIE. Thank you. That will be proof of your respect.

Pause. Everyone is embarrassed by this absurd exchange.

LUCY. Maggie has arrived early. Isn't that splendid? She walked from the turnpike.

STEPHEN. Where have you come from, Miss Tulliver?

MAGGIE. From a girl's school near Luckreth.

STEPHEN. You are a governess?

MAGGIE. No, nothing so grand. I mended the pupil's clothes.

LUCY. Maggie's plain sewing is quite exquisite. I think I must beg your help altering my dress for the charity ball.

STEPHEN. Lucy is very much involved in preparations for this ball. I confess I am beginning to feel neglected.

LUCY. Poor Stephen. You will have to be patient.

STEPHEN. I shall be glad when the idiotic thing is done with. So will most of the chaps I know. Even Doctor Kenn said the other day that he didn't like this plan of making vanity do the work of charity.

LUCY. He said that? I thought he approved of what we do.

STEPHEN. I'm sure he approves of you.

LUCY. Dr Kenn is the new vicar at St Oggs, Maggie. I know you will like him.

STEPHEN. I think him a fine fellow. He gives half his income to charity.

MAGGIE. That is indeed noble. I never heard of anyone doing such a thing.

STEPHEN. He's the only man I've ever met, who seems to have anything of the real apostle in him. (MAGGIE's *honest, open gaze has enchanted him. He sets out to break the spell.*) I only hope he doesn't think of standing for Parliament one day, or he shall find himself my adversary.

LUCY. Do you really think of doing that?

STEPHEN. Decidedly. My father's heart is set on it and gifts like mine, you know, involve great responsibilities, don't you think, Miss Tulliver?

MAGGIE. Oh yes. Such fluency and self-possession should not be wasted entirely on private occasions.

STEPHEN. You are very perceptive. You have discovered already that I am talkative and impudent.

MAGGIE *walks to the window.*

MAGGIE. I can hear the Floss from here. You are so lucky to have the river at the bottom of your garden.

LUCY. Maggie and Tom used to live at Dorlcote Mill.

STEPHEN. Ah yes . . . your brother works for my father, I think.

MAGGIE. Yes. Do you know Tom?

STEPHEN. I'm afraid I haven't had the pleasure. (MAGGIE *looks disappointed.*) I wonder, Miss Tulliver, if you would like us all to go for a row on the river, during your stay? I would be happy to oblige.

LUCY. Oh, Maggie! Stephen is an excellent oarsman.

MAGGIE. Thank you. It is a long time since I was on the river. There is nothing I would like better.

Scene Twenty-Four

In MAGGIE's *bedroom.* MAGGIE *puts her case down, but is too agitated to unpack. She sits and then stands again and begins to pace the room. Her eyes and cheeks glow, her hands are clasped.* SECOND MAGGIE *appears and watches.*

SECOND MAGGIE. We should go to bed.

> SECOND MAGGIE *kneels and prays.* THIRD MAGGIE *begins to unpack, but* FIRST MAGGIE *enters, dancing and joyful.*

THIRD MAGGIE. I feel as if I've walked into a book. Into a dream. Everything is so beautiful here; the very air seems charged with delight . . . and love . . . I had given up believing such places exist.

SECOND MAGGIE. We should go to bed.

THIRD MAGGIE (*sharply*). What are you doing here?

> FIRST *and* SECOND MAGGIE*s leave.* LUCY *enters.*

LUCY. Maggie, tell me what you think of him.

MAGGIE. Oh, I think you should humiliate him a little. A lover should not be so at ease. He ought to tremble more.

LUCY. Tremble at me! You think he is conceited.

MAGGIE. A little over-confident.

LUCY. Sometimes, when he's away, I think he can't possibly love me, but I never doubt it when he's with me again. We're not engaged, you know.

MAGGIE. Ah. So if I disapprove of him, you can give him up.

LUCY. You don't disapprove, do you? You don't dislike him?

MAGGIE. Lucy. Am I in the habit of seeing such charming people, that I should be very difficult to please?

> LUCY *is delighted. They embrace.*

LUCY. You know, one of the things I most admire in him is that he makes a greater friend of Phillip Wakem than anyone. (*There is a change in* MAGGIE*'s face.*) I'm sorry. Does it hurt you to hear the name?

MAGGIE. No. No. I've liked Phillip Wakem since I was a little girl. He was very good to me.

LUCY. So you won't mind if he visits? He and Stephen have the only decent voices in St Oggs. Our musical evenings would suffer without him. Oh please. I remember what a wild state of joy you used to be in when the singers came round. We can have all the songs you used to love.

MAGGIE. I don't know . . . I would have to ask Tom. I couldn't see him without his leave.

LUCY. Is Tom such a tyrant as that?

MAGGIE. Lucy, I promised Tom, solemnly, that I would not speak to Phillip again without his consent.

LUCY. But I've never heard anything so unreasonable. (*Pause.*) You have secrets from me, and I have none from you.

MAGGIE. I would like to tell you about Phillip. I have needed to tell someone.

Scene Twenty-Five

In TOM's *room at* BOB JAKIN's. TOM *and* MAGGIE *stand in tense silence.*

MAGGIE. Tom? Please say something. I only ask because Lucy wishes it. I would only see him in the presence of other people.

TOM. Do you really pretend what I say would make a difference? You will do exactly what you want in the end.

MAGGIE. That is unfair.

TOM. As you told me, very bluntly, after father's death, you wish to be independent.

MAGGIE. Is that so hard to understand?

TOM. I wished my sister to be a lady and I would always have taken care of you as my father desired.

MAGGIE. Dear Tom, I know that you would do a great deal for me . . . but you don't seem to realise how differently we feel about things.

TOM. Oh, I realise only too well – when you can entertain the idea of Phillip Wakem as a lover, a husband, after all that . . . I realise how differently we feel.

MAGGIE. I know there could never be any question of our marrying. Not as things stand. I am not totally unaware of what is right and wrong.

TOM. But you do not have the strength to resist what is wrong.

MAGGIE. That is not true.

TOM. Isn't it? (MAGGIE *begins to cry.* TOM *softens.*) I don't want to overstrain matters, Maggie. I think, all things considered, it would be best for you to see Phillip Wakem if Lucy wishes it. But if you begin to think of him as anything more than a friend, you will lose me forever.

FIRST MAGGIE *enters, running to* TOM *and flinging her arms around him.*

FIRST MAGGIE. Oh Tom, I do love you, so much. I won't be naughty I promise I won't. Please be good to me, Tom.

TOM (*smiling and allowing her to kiss him*). All right, Magsie. All right.

FIRST MAGGIE *leaves.*

THIRD MAGGIE. I may turn out better than you expect.

TOM. I hope you will.

MAGGIE. And may I come one day and make tea for you, and meet Bob's new wife?

TOM. Yes. Off you go now. Be a good girl. (*She kisses him and goes to the door.*) Maggie.

MAGGIE. Yes.

TOM. There may be a chance that I will get the mill back. I have persuaded Guest and Co. to purchase it and allow me to manage it.

MAGGIE. That's wonderful news. (*Taking his hands.*) Come and have dinner tonight, with me and Lucy. She would love to see you.

TOM. I am sure there are other people Lucy would much rather see. And besides, I have too much to do.

She goes. TOM *is upset and angry with himself for not being able to respond to her kindness.*

Scene Twenty-Six

In the drawing room at LUCY*'s.* STEPHEN *is just finishing a song.* LUCY *and* MAGGIE *lay down their knitting and sewing to applaud.*

LUCY. Bravo! Bravo! Hasn't he a splendid voice?

MAGGIE. Neither of us can be judges of that. You are not impartial, and I think any barrel-organ splendid.

STEPHEN. I suppose you would prefer a tenor, Miss Tulliver, warbling sentimental love and constancy.

MAGGIE. Not at all. I enjoy all music. Even the loud variety.

STEPHEN. I think that decidedly vicious. I put a great deal of effort into that ditty.

MAGGIE. There was certainly a quantity of air involved.

LUCY. Really! You two are quite incorrigible

MAGGIE. Please sing another song, Mr Guest. I enjoyed it enormously.

STEPHEN. That sounds dangerously close to a compliment.

Their eyes meet. Both look away. It is compromising to feel the effect they have on one another.

LUCY *and* STEPHEN *go. It is evening.* MAGGIE *takes up her knitting again. She is using scarlet wool. Music.* SECOND MAGGIE *enters and hovers behind her.*

THIRD MAGGIE. I don't know why you're here; I'm doing nothing you could disapprove of.

She carries on knitting. SECOND MAGGIE *watches her.* STEPHEN *enters. He looks sheepish. He is carrying a book under his arm.* MAGGIE *rises.*

STEPHEN. You are surprised to see me again, Miss Tulliver. I wanted to come into the town and I got our man to row me, so I thought I would bring this music for your cousin.

MAGGIE. But Lucy is not in this evening. She said . . . do you remember? She has gone to a meeting about the ball.

STEPHEN. Ah . . . Well . . . will you give this to her?

MAGGIE. Yes.

She sits again and goes on knitting. He sits on the chair next to hers – something he has never done before. He watches her intently for quite some time.

STEPHEN. That is coming on well. (*Pause.*) We shall have a splendid sunset, I think. Will you go out and see it?

MAGGIE. I don't know. If I'm not playing cards with Uncle.

Pause.

STEPHEN. Do you like sitting alone?

MAGGIE. Would it be quite civil to say yes?

STEPHEN (*delighted with the look he has received*). It was rather a dangerous question for an intruder to ask.

Pause.

MAGGIE. I wish Lucy had not been obliged to go out. We lose our music.

STEPHEN. We shall have a new voice tomorrow night. Will you tell your cousin that our friend Phillip Wakem has come back from his trip? I saw him as I went home.

SECOND MAGGIE stands. THIRD MAGGIE starts and stands. The ball of scarlet wool falls from her lap and runs across the room.

She goes to retrieve it, but STEPHEN gets there first. He picks it up and winds it back towards her. They find themselves very close, their hands almost touching. He hands her the ball.

Music. MAGGIE, looking into STEPHEN's eyes, throws the ball again. He retrieves it and hands it back to her. She throws it again but before he can retrieve it, SECOND MAGGIE puts her foot on the wool and THIRD MAGGIE runs and picks it up. All three turn away from each other.

STEPHEN. You'll tell your cousin?

MAGGIE. Yes.

STEPHEN. That I brought the music, I mean?

MAGGIE. Yes.

STEPHEN. And about Phillip?

MAGGIE. Yes. Good evening.

He goes. MAGGIE *turns back to her chair.* SECOND
MAGGIE *is sitting there and she holds out her arms and
embraces her, as* MAGGIE *bursts into tears.*

SECOND MAGGIE. Oh, Phillip, Phillip. I wish we were
together again, so quietly in the Red Deeps. So quietly . . .

STEPHEN (*from outside*). For God's sake, Guest; what are you
doing?

Scene Twenty-Seven

In the drawing room. MAGGIE *is there.* LUCY *enters with*
PHILLIP. *He looks nervous but* MAGGIE *advances towards
him with outheld hand and tears in her eyes.*

PHILLIP (*taking her hand*). You look very well.

MAGGIE. Lucy is my fairy godmother. She does nothing but
indulge me all day long.

She smiles at LUCY, *who goes.*

MAGGIE. I told my brother I wished to see you. I asked him
to release me from the promise and he consented.

PHILLIP. Then we can at least be friends? Does Lucy know?

MAGGIE. Yes, I confided in her.

PHILLIP. I'm glad.

Pause.

MAGGIE. I can't tell you how terrible I felt . . .

PHILLIP. You don't need to say it.

MAGGIE. Oh, Phillip. We must talk together as much as we
can before I go away again.

PHILLIP. Is that inevitable?

MAGGIE. I won't be dependent on Tom. I can't be. Staying
here would only unfit me for the life I must lead.

PHILLIP. Do you not see another alternative, Maggie?

MAGGIE. Not as things are. I begin to think I will never find much happiness in loving. There is always pain mingled with it. I wish I could make a world outside it, as men do.

PHILLIP. I thought you had stopped thinking like that. I thought I had cured you of it.

MAGGIE. Yes. Yes, you are right. I wish I could have you always beside me, to guide me and teach me. So many things you told me have come true.

The thought of STEPHEN *has shot into her head. It shows.*

PHILLIP. What is the matter, Maggie? Has something happened?

MAGGIE. No. Nothing. Nothing. You used to say I would feel the effect of my starved life, as you called it, and I do. I am too eager in my enjoyment of . . . luxuries. Tell me of you, Phillip.

PHILLIP. I still paint and draw a great deal. I have a studio now, at the top of my father's house. It is very private.

MAGGIE. I had an attic once. It was the only place I could be really myself.

PHILLIP. Maggie, I could be beside you always. If you wished me to be.

Scene Twenty-Eight

In the drawing room. STEPHEN *and* PHILLIP *come to the end of a duet.* MAGGIE *and* LUCY *are enraptured.*

LUCY. More, more! Something spirited again. Maggie always says she likes a great rush of sound.

STEPHEN. You sang exceptionally, Phil.

LUCY. You did.

STEPHEN. You are an enviable fellow, a true artist. When I sing, my mind wanders dreadfully. But then that has been observed in men of a great administrative capacity, I believe – a tendency to predominance of the reflective powers. Haven't you observed that, Miss Tulliver?

MAGGIE. I have observed a tendancy to predominance.

PHILLIP notices the look exchanged.

LUCY. Come, come. Music, more music. We can discuss each other's qualities another time.

PHILLIP begins to sing 'I Love Thee Still'. The others listen. MAGGIE becomes embarrassed. She goes to get her wool, but STEPHEN anticipates her want and passes it to her.

MAGGIE (*not looking at him*). Thank you.

STEPHEN. Is there not a draught here? Would you like to move nearer to the fire?

MAGGIE. No thank you.

Their eyes meet. PHILLIP has witnessed all. He stops singing and looks down. Then continues, but his heart has sunk.

LUCY, PHILLIP and STEPHEN leave. The lights change. FIRST MAGGIE enters, in a state of high excitement, carrying a black brocade dress. She helps THIRD MAGGIE to put it on. THIRD MAGGIE looks at herself in the mirror.

FIRST MAGGIE. It's beautiful, beautiful.

SECOND MAGGIE enters.

SECOND MAGGIE. Why are you dressed like that?

THIRD MAGGIE. For the charity ball.

SECOND MAGGIE (*grabbing her and trying to tear it from her*). Take it off.

THIRD MAGGIE. It's an old dress of Aunt Pullet's.

SECOND MAGGIE. Take it off.

THIRD MAGGIE. There will be ladies in shining new silks. I have to wear something. (*She pushes her away.*)

FIRST MAGGIE (*holding out her hand*). Your Majesty . . .

SECOND MAGGIE. Take it off.

THIRD MAGGIE. No.

She turns away as the grand music of the ball begins and the stage is filled with people dancing. FIRST MAGGIE dances alone. SECOND MAGGIE dances with DR KENN. STEPHEN and LUCY dance together. A man approaches MAGGIE and bows but she declines to dance and he withdraws.

LUCY. Why doesn't Maggie dance? She has had so many offers. You must go and ask her. She would dance with you.

STEPHEN. I'm not at all sure she would.

PHILLIP enters the upper platform which has become the gallery. He watches MAGGIE.

She glances up and sees him just as STEPHEN appears by her side.

STEPHEN. Maggie.

MAGGIE. Where is Lucy?

STEPHEN. Will you dance with me?

MAGGIE. No. No, I'm sorry.

STEPHEN. Are you angry with me? What have I done? Do look at me.

MAGGIE. Please go away.

She glances again at the gallery. STEPHEN follows her eyes and sees PHILLIP. He realises there must be something between them. He goes up to the gallery.

STEPHEN. Are you studying for a portrait, Phil?

PHILLIP. I have been studying expression.

STEPHEN. Miss Tulliver's? It's rather of the moody order tonight. I have been snubbed as usual. I seldom have the honour to please her.

PHILLIP. What a hypocrite you are.

Both men stand and face each other. PHILLIP leaves. STEPHEN runs down the steps and sweeps MAGGIE off her feet into the waltz. She manages to keep up with him, clumsily at first, but then the music and lights change, and the other dancers become shadows and STEPHEN and MAGGIE glide perfectly in each other's arms. They stop.

MAGGIE. We must go back in. We will be missed.

STEPHEN says nothing, but holds out his hand to her. Slowly she takes it. He suddenly showers her hand and arm with kisses. She snatches her hand away.

How dare you? What right have I given you to insult me? (*She runs from him. He follows her, shocked.*) Leave me alone. (*He goes.*)

She runs into DR KENN.

Father . . .

DOCTOR. Miss Tulliver, you are finding our party fatiguing, I'm afraid.

MAGGIE. Yes.

DOCTOR. I hope I am going to have you as a permanent parishioner now.

MAGGIE. No. I will go to a new situation.

DOCTOR. I was hoping you would remain among your friends.

MAGGIE (*with great emphasis*). I must go.

DOCTOR. I understand. But that will not prevent our meeting again, I hope – if I can be of service to you.

Scene Twenty-Nine

In the drawing room. THIRD MAGGIE *stands very still.*

FIRST MAGGIE *enters and runs about, panicking as she did about the rabbits.*

FIRST MAGGIE. Oh please don't let it be true. Please, please . . .

THIRD MAGGIE *takes, almost rips, the ball dress off.* FIRST MAGGIE *helps her into her old dress.* LUCY *enters.*

LUCY. Maggie, you can't go away. Not now.

MAGGIE. I have to. Please don't try to dissuade me. I had the offer of a situation yesterday.

LUCY. But what about Phillip . . . I thought everything was going to be so happy – you and Phillip, Stephen and I . . .

MAGGIE. I have to consider Tom's feelings.

LUCY. But I could talk to him.

MAGGIE. No. Thank you.

LUCY. Maggie, is it that you don't love Phillip enough to marry him? Tell me . . .

Pause.

MAGGIE. I would choose to marry Phillip. I think it would be the best and highest lot for me. But I must go. Don't press me to stay, dear Lucy. Please.

LUCY *goes.* PHILLIP *enters.*

PHILLIP. Maggie, I have told my father everything. He will not stand between us.

MAGGIE. Phillip, I am going away at the end of the week.

Pause.

PHILLIP. So the future will never join onto the past. That book is quite closed?

MAGGIE. No. That book will never be closed. I desire no future that will break the ties of the past. But there is my brother – I could do nothing that would divide me from him.

PHILLIP. Maggie, look at me. Is that the only reason that would keep us apart forever? The only reason?

MAGGIE. The only reason.

Scene Thirty

In the mill. TOM *and* MAGGIE, MRS TULLIVER, AUNT *and* UNCLE GLEGG *enter. They look about them.* MRS TULLIVER *and* MAGGIE *strip the dust sheets from the old furniture.*

MRS TULLIVER. What news, eh, Sister? What news! I never thought I'd be back in the old place, again.

MR GLEGG. Why you're a big man now, Tom and carry all before you. You'll buy the place from Mr Guest one day and have it for your own, I'll be bound. You won't stop half way up the hill.

MRS GLEGG. But I hope he'll bear it in mind as it's his mother's family as he owes it to. There was never failures, nor wastefulness in our family.

MR GLEGG. But who would ha' thought Wakem 'ud sell? Eh?

MRS GLEGG. Well, Bessy, I shall give my nephy some
   serviceable sheets and I hope he'll lie down in 'em and
   think of his aunt. Though I must say, it's fine work to be
   dividing my linen before I die.

MRS TULLIVER. I'm sure it was no wish o' mine, Sister, as
   I should lie awake o' nights thinking o' my best-bleached
   linen all over the county.

MRS GLEGG. But I shan't be giving Maggie any more o' my
   dresses, if she's to go into service when she might stay here
   and keep me company, if you didn't want her.

MR GLEGG. Nonsense, nonsense. Don't let us hear o' you
   taking a place again, Maggie. Why, you must ha' picked up
   half a dozen sweethearts at the ball. In't there one of 'em
   the right sort of article? Eh? Eh?

MRS GLEGG. Mr Glegg, if you're going to be undelicate, let
   me know.

   They go. TOM *and* MAGGIE *remain.*

TOM. Magsie, come and live with me and Mother. It's not too
   late to change your mind.

MAGGIE. Oh, Tom . . . (*She hugs him.*) Thank you for saying
   that. But I have to go.

   TOM *turns and goes.*

Scene Thirty-One

MAGGIE *is standing by the Floss, staring at the water. We can
hear it lapping against the banks.* STEPHEN *approaches.*
MAGGIE *sees his reflection and immediately darts away.*

STEPHEN. You are angry with me for coming.

MAGGIE. I did not think you would wish to insult me further
   by forcing an interview on me in this way. Kindly let me
   return to the house.

STEPHEN. Of course, it is of no consequence what a man has
   to suffer. It is only your woman's dignity which you care
   about. As if it were not enough that I am caught up in this,

that I'm mad with love for you, but you must treat me like a
coarse brute who would willingly offend you. And when, if
I had my own choice, I should ask you to take my hand, my
fortune, my whole life and do what you want with them.
I know I forgot myself. I hate myself for having done it but
I repented immediately. The worst pain I could have is to
have pained you. I would give the world to recall the error.

MAGGIE. You must not say these things. I must not hear them.

STEPHEN. Look at me: see what a hunted devil I am. I have
been riding thirty miles every day to get away from the
thought of you.

MAGGIE. I don't think any evil of you. I do forgive you. But
please go away.

STEPHEN. I can't go away from you.

MAGGIE. It is wicked . . . base . . . think of Lucy . . .

STEPHEN. I do think of her. If I did not . . .

MAGGIE. And I have other ties.

STEPHEN. You are engaged to Phillip Wakem? Is it so?

MAGGIE. I consider myself engaged to him. I don't mean to
marry anyone else.

Pause.

STEPHEN. Tell me then, that you don't care for me. Tell me
that you love someone better. Tell me and I'll go. (*She can't
answer.*) Come out in the boat with me, Maggie.

MAGGIE. I can't. It is out of the question.

STEPHEN. Do you remember, you said how you yearned to be
on the river? We will not be long together. Let us have these
last moments.

*He takes her hand. She does not resist. Music. He leads her,
like someone blind, to the boat. He arranges the cushions
and opens a parasol above her head. They are afloat.*
STEPHEN *rows and the air is filled with the rhythmic
sound of the oars and birds in flight. Everything is very slow
and languid. Occasionally,* STEPHEN *utters a quiet
exclamation of love. Then he lays down the oars and sits
back. The boat glides.*

The music changes. The sky grows dark. Suddenly MAGGIE
sits up in alarm and looks about.

MAGGIE. Are we past Luckreth? We should have stopped
there.

STEPHEN (*in a dreamy absent tone*). Yes – a long way.

MAGGIE. Oh, my God . . . we won't get home for hours. Oh
God, help me . . . Lucy . . .

STEPHEN. Maggie, let us never go home again until we are
married. Look . . . the tide has carried us away because we
belong to each other. It will take us to Torby, we can get a
carriage to York and then to Scotland and never stop until
we are bound together.

MAGGIE. Let me go! How could you do this? You knew we
had come too far. How could you bring me to this?

STEPHEN. I didn't notice that we had passed Luckreth until it
was too late. You clearly don't love me enough. If you did,
nothing else would matter. I will stop the boat and try to get
you out. I'll tell Lucy I was mad and you shall be clear of
me forever.

MAGGIE. No. I'm sorry . . . I'm . . . I have been as weak as
you. I would always care what happened to you.

STEPHEN. Oh Maggie, my darling, my dearest love . . . marry
me, just say the word.

MAGGIE. No . . . no, I would rather die than fall into that
temptation.

STEPHEN. It would be wrong to deny our love. Do you not
see how strong it is? How can we go back to those others,
knowing how we feel about each other?

MAGGIE. Oh Stephen, please, please don't urge me; help
me . . . help me because I love you.

*He takes her in his arms and kisses her. Her resolution
cracks. She sinks into the temptation and lets go.*

STEPHEN. You are mine, now. Lie back my darling, rest. I
will row to Torby. Everything is all right now, Maggie.
Everything is all right.

MAGGIE *closes her eyes and sleeps. But she dreams. We*